A CONTEMPORARY APPROACH TO CYBERCRIME

TANSIF UR REHMAN
SYED MUHAMMAD IRFAN
GHULAM DASTGIR

ELIVA PRESS

TANSIF UR REHMAN
SYED MUHAMMAD IRFAN
GHULAM DASTGIR

The internet is conceivably today's most compelling innovative development as well as it proceeds to change everyday life for almost everyone globally. Billions of individuals are plugged into the internet, in addition to thousands additional enter the online world each day. Cybercrime's pace globally is on a high rise. It is an offense that is even harder to identify and resolve as compared to traditional crimes. The respective work which has been carried out regarding the very notion of cybercrime has its significance in helping as well as exploring this dilemma via a multifaceted as well as contemporaneous approach. Authors intention is to critically analyze the multifaceted dimensions of cybercrime with respect to encompassing issues. This work can serve as a valuable resource with regards to contemporary approaches to cybercrime.

Published: Eliva Press SRL
Address: MD-2060, bd.Cuza-Voda, 1/4, of. 21 Chişinău, Republica
Moldova
Email: info@elivapress.com
Website: www.elivapress.com

ISBN: 978-1-63648-009-1

Table of contents

Chapter 1: Conceptual Basis of Cybercrime

Abstract

The internet is conceivably today's most compelling innovative development as well as it proceeds to change everyday life for almost every one globally. Billions of individuals are plugged into the internet, in addition to thousands additional enter the online world each day. Not merely has the internet revolutionized the way people connect and learn, it has eternally changed the way people live across the globe. At the same time, as internet as well as computer advances persist to thrive, offenders have originated ways to utilize these innovations in the same way as an instrument intended for their criminal acts. In social science research, social theories are of great significance. Social facts without a theoretical direction are like a snuffed out candle that is unable to determine the path of its bearer. Social theories contribute in the development of sound scientific foundations for resolving issues in any social inquiry. Theories guide our observations of the world. A theory is never proven, though; the research can only provide support for a theory. However, research also can reveal weakness in theory and force researchers to modify the theory or develop a new and more comprehensive one. Digital technology has a very fast impact and has numerous challenges. The respective work which has been carried out regarding the very notion of cybercrime has its significance in helping as well as exploring this dilemma via a multifaceted theoretical approach.

Keywords: behavior, cybercrime, cyberworld, hacking, Routine Activity, Self-Control, Social Learning, theories.

2

Introduction

Generally, a theory is an assumption or thought. Social theory explains a notion in a brief manner and it comprises of some logical reasons that are collected over a period of time. However, the definition of social theory varies according to context and methodologies. A social theory may not be necessarily based on everyone's opinion, as it might be a statement irrespective of the fact that what people actually think about it. Thus, a social theory is a proposition, an opinion which helps researchers to explore the unexplored situation that exists and is available to be observed.

Theory and research both are important notions. Theory provides the basic structure of propositions and research provides the technique and method to fit the theory in a particular context. It also helps to bring modifications regarding the existing theories (Sarantakos, 2013).

In spite of the fact that, these theories were formerly intended to elucidate traditional crimes, they can still be functional regarding the very notion of cybercrime in today's world. The presented research has incorporated sociological theories and the respective research builds a context around these theories.

It is sometime tempting to downplay cybercrime, painting it always being the action of a lone individual, but while this is true of some crimes, the reality of cybercrime as a whole is very different (Benson & McAlaney, 2019; Johansen, 2020; Troia, 2020; Yar & Steinmetz, 2019). In contemporary era, several thousand groups are dedicated to cybercrime because of the rewards attached to it (Austin, 2020; Gillespie, 2019; Leukfeldt & Holt, 2019). It is clearly evident that as people become more dependent on technology, they become easier targets of cybercrime (Hudak, 2019; Martellozzo & Jane, 2017; Steinberg, 2019), as it also could evolve to bring about new problems (Hufnagel & Moiseienko, 2019; Marion & Twede, 2020). It is also important to realize to what extent it is understood by people that either they are really a victim or can be the victim of a cybercrime (Abaimov & Martellini, 2020; Marsh & Melville, 2019).

It is important to realize to what extent cybercrime is understood by people that either they are really a victim or can be the victim of a cybercrime (Azevedo, 2019; Carlson, 2019; Steinberg, 2019). For example, the sending of emails trying to influence people to enter their bank detail is illegal, but almost every one with an email address will have received an email asking them to confirm their bank details (Bancroft, 2019; Bandler & Merzon, 2020).Another problem is the issue in identifying victims of cybercrime are those situations where people do not know that they have been victimized (Edwards 2019; Graham & Smith, 2019; Hutchings, 2013; Sangster, 2020). Most users of the computer will be aware of the need to install firewall and antivirus software (Littler & Lee, 2020; Schober & Schober; 2019). It is often rare for someone to be told that the program has stopped a virus or potential hack (Kim, 2018; Lavorgna, 2020; Willems, 2019).

Focus of the Research

The respective research encompasses the enlisted sociological theories with reference to behavior encompassing cybercrime in the contemporary era.

1. Routine Activity Theory

2. Self-Control Theory

3. Social Learning Theory

Research Methodology

The basis of the chapter is based on the theoretical framework. At this point, a descriptive research methodology was used. Descriptive research "is more concerned with what it is, rather than how or why it is something and aims to define a phenomenon and its properties" (Cozby, 1997; Nassaji 2015, p.129).

Routine Activity Theory

Routine Activity Theory was initially articulated by Lawrence E. Cohen and M. Felson in 1979 and further systematically elaborated by Felson. This theory is quoted to a great extent by several noteworthy authors. It is one of the influential theory that possesses authoritative theoretical entity in the field of criminological sciences.

The centre of the Routine Activity Theory is understanding the crime as a subset of possible outcomes of some activity. Significance of time and space are featured as the state of being mutually or reciprocally interconnected. Interrelationship of humans and their environment is properly discussed along with its implications. This theory is different to other proposed theories of criminal activity which focus on sociobiological and psychological   aspects that actuate the person for crime.

According to Cohen and Felson (1979), this theory is a noticeable effort to determine the causes of criminality, unlawful activities, and their occurring patterns. It is helpful in evaluating the variation of crime rate if assessed statistically over time on large scale.

Tilley (2009) further explained in his seminal work that, Routine Activity Theory relies on the occurrence of activities that are unlawful and criminological, instead of investigating the intentions of criminals.

This theory provides a logical framework for the crime analysis or assay for specifically and particularized offenses. It helps the authorities to implement the definite course or method of actions in the light of given theory. The objective, that remains, of the policies is to change the unavoidable factors that ensure the commencement of crime possible, while ultimately helps in averting the crimes.

Globalization and the evolution of contemporary societies have eventually made people more vulnerable to criminal threats. Extensive surveys and reports have already been published by different authors in this sphere. Women used to remain at home, while breadwinners who were usually males went out from home for longer hours. Since, the induction of women in workplaces and their passion for higher education increased the possibilities of intrusion for offender for empty homes.

Likewise, long visits outside the city or country and post of pictures on social media, online games where children came across with strangers, private information shared online, etc. increased the vulnerability for victims and opportunity for the offenders.

Furthermore, the technological advancement and availability of small home appliances, like televisions, stereo equipment, laptops, mobiles, etc., which are higher in monetary value and lower in weight and easy to carry, opened the doors of new opportunities for offender to commit crime easily and disappear. Introduction of ATMs all around the cities, increase in banking activities, carrying of mobile and other light weighted devices, ultimately increased the likelihood of being looted.

Briefly, it can be stated that increasing number of available light weighted valuable things, vulnerability to intrude homes, continuous internet connectivity, least awareness regarding cybercrime, children vulnerability to online paedophiles, ineffective policing is producing a lot of suitable victims. Humans are suffering from incapable guardianship to prevent crimes, whether in physical world or cyber space. Thus, an encompassing environment of numerous opportunities for offenders of all types exists.

By experimentation and examination researchers have compiled enough support for employing the standards and principles of Routine Activity Theory to the study of online crimes (van Wilsem, 2011; Reyns, 2013). Furthermore, its implication in the victimology seems evident as the behavior of victims are repetitive and predictive. Evidences are strong enough to establish presumption of victimization to **three** core elements.

1. Motivated criminal or offender

2. Lack of competent guardianship

3. Vulnerable victims

The motivated criminal or offender is a person who has the intention of committing crime, if the situation is suitable and safe. Competent guardianship refers to anything that hinder the criminal to execute his/her intention, i.e. a vulnerable target (e.g., firewall, IT security experts, etc.). Vulnerable victim is used to define something that is valuable and precious for criminal or offender. (e.g., personal identity information, bank account details, classified data, etc.).

Online activities all around the world has been growing speedily, which is ultimately facilitating the criminals to exploit the available vulnerabilities. There exists whole new opportunities and forum for cyber criminals to target the unaware victim of cybercrime. Those who spend most of their time online put themselves in dangerous situations. Where there is always a probability of interaction with an offender which can cause harm to the respective victim. According to a study conducted by a US-based organization, International Centre for Missing and Exploited Children (2018), about 750,000 sexual predators worldwide are online at any given moment.

Researches concerning cybercrime reveals that risky online behavior, like careless use of internet banking, online shopping, sharing personal information, etc., make users more vulnerable to cyber criminals. The absence of able guardianship, like antivirus, firewalls, etc. is also linked to increased chances of victimization. Individuals may be the victim of cybercrime, like identity fraud, hacking, cyber bullying, phishing, DoS attacks, etc. (Reyns, 2013).

Self-Control Theory

Self-Control Theory frequently classifies within the category of General Theory of Crime to explain criminality and its causes. Self-Control Theory is one of the established philosophical and theoretical framework of scientific school of criminology. Where some theoretical versions are archetype of formal social control, for example, Deterrence and Rational Choice Theories. Some represent unconventional social control, i.e. social disorganization and collective efficacy theories. While, few relate to indirect control, e.g., Social Bond Theories, Power-Control Theories of gender and delinquency, etc.

Self-Control Theory has arguably turned out to be the most cited and authoritative notion of the Control Theory class ever since it is published by Gottfredson and Hirschi in 1990. It is evident in their work that they are reconstructing and bringing back the formal recommendations of classical school of thought aligned with positivism verified by the empirical sciences. Their vision during the development of self control and crime theory seems to achieve multiple objectives.

The Theory of Self-Control and Crime elaborate the complexity and causes of crimes as the result of impulsive behavior, i.e. instant accomplishment of desires, as well as the absence of obstruction. These aspects ultimately make the criminal event easy. During their investigative work, they realized that criminals exhibit similar traits and qualities as crime events. Furthermore, criminals were traced among those people who are unable to control their impulsiveness and always search for easy and instant gratification of their urges. Their behavior is comprised of multiple crimes along with other criminal conducts.

The Theory of Self-Control and Crimes articulate that, crime is considered as a source of achieving instant gratification. The quality or competence to be patient and holding back the craving of such instantaneous desires have definite connection with self-control. That is why, a person who has the tendency for getting involved in deviant acts lack the ability of his/her self-control. They are also impulsive most of the time, and their actions displays their trait of being thoughtlessness and inconsiderate, as they just submit beside their emotions and feelings. That is why, these type of people have risky behavior and are often inconsiderate of the consequences of their acts. Criminals with low self-control are usually self-centered, mean, and discourteous towards others (Burruss et al., 2012).

Inefficient parenting is the core reason of low self-control. It begins with primal improper socialization of parents with children. Parents give little attention and don't respect their children concerns, which ultimately inhibits the proper mental development. These children lack empathy as well as unable to control gratification, hence, impulsiveness is developed in them. Children having low self-control are being likely to get involved in criminal acts and criminal inclination remains in them as they grow older.

According to Burruss et al., (2012), Low Self-Control Theory is well applicable in common cybercrime, like software piracy. He stated that the lack of self-control has a direct affiliation with the deviant act of software piracy. As the one who is engaged in software piracy has an inability to delay gratification and lack patience to buy an original software. They neither care for the loss of software developer, nor concerned about the responsibilities they should care about. This act of software piracy may be a thrill and enjoyment for them, as it is easy to get involved.

Low Self-Control Theory undoubtedly effects cybercrime, like software piracy. Software piracy is increasingly high as the deviant peer group appreciates the activity, and has no objectionable attitude towards the unlawful act, as Social Learning Theory explains the respective phenomenon in great detail. The criterion of Low Self-Control Theory makes clear that the people with low self-control are more probable in getting engaged in criminal activities, both in cyber and physical world. The major reason is their inability to delay their instantaneous gratification.

The General Theory of Crime by Gottfredson and Hirschi's (1990), is cited frequently on the basis of observation and experience, for elucidation of crime, committed both in online and in the physical world. The affiliation of a low self-control   personalities with the deviant people can not only aggravate, but also worsen their cognition regarding cybercrime. The extended use of Information & Communication Technology (ICTs) is providing platforms to a large number of deviants to act according to their impulses.

The increase in cybercrime, like cyber harassment is discussed in the works of Bocij, (2004); Finn (2004); Holt and Bossler (2009). While, the exponential growth in pornographic material production and sites surfing is well discussed by Buzzell, Foss, and Middleton (2006).

Higgins (2005) has elaborated on the phenomenon of media piracy and online fraud. Jordan and Taylor (1998) have discussed identity theft, and these are just few examples of internet related crimes.

According to Gottfredson and Hirschi (1990) proposition, the people with low level of self-control demonstrate the characteristics of impulsiveness, lack of empathy towards others, myopic, have the tendency of risk taking, unable to delay gratification, etc. Gottfredson and Hirschi's (1990) General Theory of Crime and Association of deviant peer group elaborates the various aspects of cybercrime.

The discussion regarding relation of low self-control and affiliation of criminal peer groups are common among scholars to elaborate the crimes both conventional and cyber (e.g., Gibson & Wright, 2001; Higgins, Fell, & Wilson, 2006). Criminological studies eloquently elucidate the understandings of how low self-control influence the individuals to cyber offense. Some of the studies reckon the operational procedures specially in youth who are account for number of different cybercrime, like Taylor, Fritsch, Liederbach, and Holt (2010); and Yar (2005).

According to Wolack, Mitchell, and Finkelhor (2006), access to internet is getting easier for every one and youth is in a great number who are gaining access to the ICTs in earlier ages. There are significant findings which are quite convincing that low self-control and criminal peer group have definite effects on individuals regarding crime and delinquency both in real and cyberworld.

Social Learning Theory

Cybercrime is an emerging area for researcher in the field of criminology. There are many cited theories in criminological sciences, but limited, apart from Hollinger (1988). These respective theories inspect or inquire regarding cybercrime. Social Learning Theory is one of them, which is used by the scholars to elaborate the causes and origin of cybercrime. It facilitates in illustrating the multiple factors and behavior of cybercrime as well as cyber criminals.

Social Learning Theory by Akers (1973) was articulated initially as Differential Association Reinforcement by Burgess and Akers in 1966. They made an effort to merge the Differential Association Theory of Sutherland (1947) with the fundamental assumptions of behavioral psychology. Sutherland (1947) attempted to elaborate the proposition regarding white collar crime that was quite different from the conventional approaches of that era. At that time, most of the seminal works were focused on the subjective deficiencies of lower-class and criminals. Sutherland (1947, pp. 6-7) highlighted nine points in his proposed theory of differential association:

1. Deviant or criminal behavior is a learned behaviour.

2. It is learned due to interaction and communication with the deviants.

3. The core of the criminal behavior appears within immediate peer group.

4. When the criminal behavior is learned, it includes:

(a) Techniques and skills of   committing the offense, either difficult or easy.

(b) Distinct reason of the act and motivating factors, and mental attitude.

5. The distinct reason of the act and motivation is learned from the pseudo articulation of law as either favorable or unfavorable.

6. A person gets involve in criminal acts, because the pseudo articulation of favorable aspects of violation exceeds, while unfavorable side is minimal.

7. Differential association varies according to the frequency, time, priority and intensity.

8. The learning of deviance or criminal behavior by peer group association, either criminal or non-criminal pattern, involve all the process which includes in any other learning.

9. In spite of the fact, deviant behavior is the symbolization of their necessities and values. The behavior of non-criminals are also an expression of the same needs and values. That is why, it cannot be explained by general needs and values.

According to Akers (1998), Theory of Social Learning, crime is a behavior that is learned and embedded in peer group association, which is the root cause of the criminal duplication. That also includes pseudo articulation of right and wrong, an alibi for their act, and encouraging factors for offending. Social Learning Theory by Akers (1998) is classified as a general theory of crime and used to elucidate the wide varieties of crime and criminal behavior. There are **four** primary propositions that include:

1. Definition

2. Duplication of the act

3. Distinguished encouraging   factors

4. Discriminative peer relationship (Burruss et al., 2012)

As far as cybercrime are concerned, researchers agree that Social Learning Theory is well applicable in explaining the progressiveness and continuity of cybercrime, like software piracy. According to proposition of Burruss et al., (2012), regarding software piracy, the individual who associate with the peers, who are engaged in software piracy, usually learn and subsequently as well as willingly accept the criminal conduct. Software piracy is an act that needs technical knowledge and expertise to get success, along with the peer group from whom this expertise can be learned.

Burruss et al., (2012) further elaborated that , the criminals provide plausible, but untrue reason for their deviant conduct. They nurture the network of people and connect them, so that they teach others their pseudo justified and deviant behavior. Individuals are more prone to get engaged in deviant acts, like software piracy when they witness others success and experiences. That is how they obtain encouragement and pursue for their participation in the same criminal act.

Social Learning Theory can be used in elaborating and understanding other cybercrime as well along with software piracy. As different groups of hackers around the world have established their community, where they not only teach and share their skills, but also help others in commencement of major crimes like Distributed Denial of Services (DDoS) attacks. They have blogs and forums where they justify their deviant acts and influence other individuals to join their community. The central idea of Social Learning Theory can be concluded as, we are an average of five people with whom we spend our time mostly.

Solutions and Recommendations

1. General public awareness programs should be initiated with regards to cybercrime.

2. A strong global cyber force is required who can counter cyber threats.

3. Students should be educate regarding the vulnerabilities of cyberworld.

4. International conferences should be conducted at official level, where debates and issues pertaining the virtual world should be discussed.

5. At domestic level, special task force should be developed to ensure routine checks at the facilities where public internet access is available.

6. Websites should be under strict control regarding the offensive content.

7. Scholars should discuss cybercrime issue on different forums, specially in print as well as electronic media.

8. Criminological courses focusing on cybercrime should also be included in the regular studies of IT, social science education, law studies, business studies, etc.

Future Research Directions

Significant areas for conducting future research encompassing cybercrime via engaging qualitative, qualitative, or eclectic approach can be:

1. Criminal psychology

2. Cyberterrorism

3. Cybercrime and freedom of speech

4. Cyber security issues

5. Cyber violence

Conclusion

The use of social media is increasing exponentially, which reveals a lot of information about people, thus making them more vulnerable than ever before. Research studies into cybercrime are nominal, because the field is relatively new. As the internet is widely available, the world has become a perfect ecosystem regarding cybercrime. This research emphasized on the aspects of integrating the traditional sociological theories encompassing crime to the context with regards to which cybercrime is committed by the criminals. These respective theories also presented a point of view as well as hypothesized regarding the basic causes of crime. This equips the readers with the very fact that why certain individuals compromise themselves as well as their social environment. The centre of the Routine Activity Theory is understanding the crime as a subset of possible outcomes of some activity. Self-Control Theory posits that low self-control is a key factor underlying criminality. While, Social Learning Theory emphasizes the importance of external factors that influence criminal involvement.

References

Abaimov, S., & Martellini, M. (2020). *Cyber arms security in cyberspace.* Boca Raton, CRC
  Press. ISBN: 9780367853860

Akers, R. L. (1973). *Deviant behavior: A social learning approach.* Belmont, CA: Wadsworth
  Publishing Company, Inc.

Akers, R. L. (1998). Social learning and social structure: A general theory of crime and
deviance.   Boston, MA: Northeastern University Press

Austin, G. (2020). *National cyber emergencies: The return to civil defence.* London,
  Routledge. ISBN: 9780367360344

Azevedo, F. U. B. (2018). *Hackers exposed: Discover the secret world of cybercrime.*
  Independently published. ISBN-13: 978-1718124615

Bancroft, A. (2019). *The darknet and smarter crime: Methods for Investigating criminal
  entrepreneurs and the illicit drug economy (Palgrave studies in cybercrime and
  cybersecurity).* Cham, Palgrave Macmillan. ISBN-13: 978-3030265113

Bandler, J., & Merzon, A. (2020). *Cybercrime investigations: A comprehensive resource for
  everyone.* Boca Raton, CRC Press. ISBN-13:978-0367196233

Benson, V., & McAlaney, J. (2019). *Emerging cyber threats and cognitive vulnerabilities* (1st
  ed.). Academic Press. ISBN-13: 978-0128162033

Bocij, P. (2004). *Cyberstalking: Harassment in the internet age and how to protect your family.*
  Westport, CT: Praeger Publishers.

Burgess, R. L., & Akers, R. L. (1966). A differential association-reinforcement theory of
  criminal behavior. *Social Problems, 14(2),* 128-147.

Burruss, G. W., Bossler, A. M., & Holt, T. J. (2012). Assessing the mediation of a fuller social learning model on low self-control's influence on software piracy. *Crime & Delinquency, 59,* 1157-1184.

Buzzell, B., Foss, D., & Middleton, Z. (2006). Explaining use of online pornography: A test of self-control theory and opportunities for deviance. *Journal of Criminal Justice and Popular Culture, 13*(2), 96-116 .

Carlson, C. T. (2019). *How to manage cybersecurity risk: A security leader's roadmap with open fair.* Universal Publishers. ISBN-13: 978-1627342766

Cohen, L. E., & Felson, M. (1979). Social change and crime rate trends: A routine activity approach. *American Sociological Review, 44*(4), 588-608.

Cozby, P. C. (1997). *Methods in behavioral research.* Houston, Texas: Mayfield Publishing Company.

Edwards, G. (2019). *Cybercrime investigators* (1st ed.). Hoboken, Wiley. ISBN-13: 978-1119596288

Finn, J. (2004). A survey of online harassment at a university campus. *Journal of Interpersonal Violence, 19(4),* 468-83.

Graham, R. S., & Smith, S. K. (2019). *Cybercrime and digital deviance* (1st ed.). New York, Routledge. ISBN: 9780815376316

Gibson, C., & Wright, J. (2001). Low self-control and coworker delinquency: A research note. *Journal of Criminal Justice, 29,* 483-492.

Gillespie, A. A. (2019). *Cybercrime: Key issues and debates*, London, Routledge. ISBN: 9781351010283

Gottfredson, M., & Hirschi, T. (1990). *A general theory of crime.* Stanford, CA: Stanford
  University Press.

Higgins, G. E. (2005). Can low self-control help with the understanding of the software piracy
  problem?. *Deviant Behavior, 26*(1), 1-24.

Higgins, G. E., Fell, B. D., & Wilson, A. L. (2006). Digital piracy: Assessing the
  contributions of an integrated self-control theory and social learning theory using   structural
  equation modeling. *Criminal Justice Studies, 19*(1),   3-22.

Hollinger, R. C. (1988). Computer hackers follow a Guttman-like progression. *Sociology and
  Social Research, 72,* 199-200.

Holt, T. J., & Bossler, A. M. (2009). Examining the applicability of lifestyle-routine activities
  theory for cybercrime victimization.   *Deviant Behavior, 30*(1), 1-25.

Hudak, H. C. (2019). *Cybercrime (Privacy in the digital age).* North Star Editions. ISBN-13:
  978-1644940815

Hufnagel, S., & Moiseienko, A. (2019). *Criminal networks and law enforcement: Global
  perspectives on illegal enterprise.* London, Routledge.

Hutchings, A. (2013). *Theory and crime: Does it compute?.* Australia: Griffith University.

International Monetary Fund (2020). *World economic outlook database.*
  https://www.imf.org/external/pubs/ft/weo/2019/02/weodata/index.aspx

International Centre for Missing and Exploited Children. (2018, June 17).
  https://tribune.com.pk/story/1736571/3-grooming-gateway-child-sex-trafficking-seducing-
  moves-online

Johansen, G. (2020). *Digital forensics and incident response: Incident response techniques and procedures to respond to modern cyber threats.* Birmingham, Packt Publishing. ISBN-13: 978-1838649005

Jordan, T., & Taylor, P. (1998). A sociology of hackers. *The Sociological Review, 40* (1), 1-25.

Kim, P. (2018). *The hacker playbook 3: Practical guide to penetration testing.* Independently published. ISBN-13: 978-1980901754

Lavorgna, A. (2020). *Cybercrimes: Critical issues in a global context.* Springer. ISBN-13: 978-1352009118

Leukfeldt, R., & Holt, T. J. (2019). *The human factor of cybercrime.* London, Routledge. ISBN-13: 978-1138624696

Littler, M., & Lee, B. (2020). *Digital extremisms: Readings in violence, radicalisation and extremism in the online space.* Cham, Springer Nature Switzerland AG. ISBN13: 9783030301378

Marion, N. E., & Twede, J. (2020). *Cybercrime: An encyclopedia of digital crime.* Santa Barbara, ABC-CLIO. ISBN-13: 978-1440857348

Marsh, B., & Melville, G. (2019). *Crime, justice and the media.* London, Routledge. ISBN: 9780429432194

Martellozzo, E., & Jane, E. A. (2017). *Cybercrime and its victims.* London, Routledge.

Nassaji, H. (2015). Qualitative and descriptive research: Data type versus data analysis. *Language Teaching Research, 19*(2), 129-132.

Reyns, B. W. (2013). Online routines and identity theft victimization: Further explaining routine activity theory beyond direct-control offenses. *Journal of Research in Crime and Delinquency, 50*(2), 216-238.

Sarantakos, S. (2013). *Social research.* NY: Palgrave Macmillan.

Schober, S. N., & Schober, C. W. (2019). *Cybersecurity is everybody's business: Solve the security puzzle for your small business and home.* ScottSchober.com Publishing.

Sutherland, E. H. (1947). *Principles of criminology* (4th ed.). Philadelphia, PA: J. B. Lippincott & Co.

Steinberg, J. (2019). *Cybersecurity for dummies (For dummies computer/tech).* Hoboken, John Wiley & Sons. ISBN: 9781119560326

Taylor, R. W., Fritsch, E. J., Liederbach, J., & Holt, T. J. (2010). *Digital crime and digital terrorism* (2nd ed.). Upper Saddle River, NJ: Pearson Prentice Hall.

Tilley, N. (2009). *Crime prevention.* Cullompton, UK: Willan Publishing.

Troia, V. (2020). *Hunting cyber criminals: A hacker's guide to online Intelligence gathering tools and techniques.* Indianapolis, Wiley. ISBN-13: 978-1119540922

van Wilsem. J. (2011). Worlds tied together? Online and non-domestic routine activities and their impact on digital and traditional threat victimization. *European Journal of Criminology, 8*(2), 115-127.

Willems, E. (2019). *Cyberdanger: Understanding and guarding against cybercrime.* Springer International Publishing. ISBN:978-3-030-04531-9

Wolack, J., Mitchell, K., & Finkelhor, D. (2006). Online victimization of youth,

   Washington, D.C.: National Center for Missing & Exploited Children.

Yar, M. (2005). Computer hacking: Just another case of juvenile delinquency? *The Howard*

   Journal, 44(4), 387-399.

Yar, M., & Steinmetz, K. F. (2019). *Cybercrime and society* (3rd ed.). SAGE Publications   Ltd.

   ISBN-13: 978-1526440648

Additional Readings

1. Abadinsky, H. (2007). *Organized crime.* Toronto: Nelson Education.

2. Akers, R. L. (1977). *Deviant behavior: A social learning approach* (2nd ed.). Belmont, CA:

    Wadsworth Pub. Co.

3. Akers, R. L. (2011). *Social learning and social structure: A general theory of crime and*

    deviance. NJ: Transaction Publishers.

4. Barak, G. (1998). *Integrating criminologies.* Boston: Allyn and Bacon.

5. Bartollas, C. (2005). *Juvenile delinquency* (7th ed.). Boston: Allyn & Bacon.

6. Brantingham, P., & Brantingham, P. (2008). Crime pattern theory. *Environmental*

    criminology and crime analysis, 78.

7. Cloward, R., & Ohlin, L. (2013). *Delinquency and opportunity: A study of delinquent*

    gangs. Routledge.

8. Cornish, D. B., & Clarke, R. V. (Eds.). (2014). *The reasoning criminal: Rational choice*

    perspectives on offending. NJ: Transaction Publishers.

9. Downes, D. M., & Rock, P. (2011). *Understanding deviance: A guide to the sociology of crime and rule-breaking.* Oxford, UK: Oxford University Press.

10. Hutchings, A. (2013). *Theory and crime: Does it compute?.* Australia: Griffith University.

Key Terms

1. **Cybercrime:** The use of a computer to commit a crime.

2. **Cyberworld:** The world of inter-computer communication.

3. **Hacking:** To gain unauthorized access to data in a system or computer.

4. **Self-Control:** The ability to regulate one's emotions, thoughts, and behavior.

5. **Social Learning:** Individuals learn from one another, via observation, imitation, and modeling.

Chapter 2: Contemporary Issues in Cybercrime

Abstract

The internet is conceivably today's most compelling innovative development as well as it proceeds to change everyday life for almost everyone globally. Billions of individuals are plugged into the internet, in addition to thousands additional enter the online world each day. Not merely has the internet revolutionized the way people connect and learn, it has eternally changed the way people live across the globe. At the same time, as internet as well as computer advances persist to thrive, offenders have originated ways to utilize these innovations in the same way as an instrument intended for their criminal acts. Cybercrime's pace globally is on a high rise. It is an offense that is even harder to identify and resolve as compared to traditional crimes in the international context. Cybercrime cells all around the world receives thousands of complaints on a daily basis. Cyber criminals are honing their skills, while consumers remain unconcerned. Cyber criminals are innovative, organized, and far sophisticated. They employ their tools effectively, working harder, and focused to uncover new vulnerabilities as well as escape detection. The ICTs are opening a whole new world of opportunities for criminals and the risk remains largely unknown. This chapter was formed by a systematic review method.

Keywords: *cyberterrorism, cyber fraud, USA, China, EU, systematic review.*

Introduction

Cybercrime can be defined in multiple ways; in the broadest sense, any offense involving a computer system may be included in this category. Few definitions encompassing the subject matter are cited.

According to Merriam-Webster (2020), "Criminal activity (such as fraud, theft, or distribution of child pornography) committed using a computer especially to illegally access, transmit, or manipulate data". While, in accordance with Oxford Advanced Learner's Dictionary (2020), "Crime that is committed using the internet, for example by stealing somebody's personal or bank details or by infecting their computer with a virus".

"Cybercrime is a crime committed by means of computers or the internet" (Collins English Dictionary, 2020). While according to The Chambers Dictionary (2020), "Criminal activity or a crime that involves the internet, a computer system, or computer technology".

Encyclopedia Britannica (2020) states, "Cybercrime, the use of a computer as an instrument to further illegal ends, such as committing fraud, trafficking in child pornography and intellectual property, stealing identities, or violating privacy. Cybercrime, especially through the Internet, has grown in importance as the computer has".

It is sometime tempting to downplay cybercrime, painting it always being the action of a lone individual, but while this is true of some crimes, the reality of cybercrime as a whole is very different (Benson & McAlaney, 2019; Johansen, 2020; Troia, 2020; Yar & Steinmetz, 2019). In contemporary era, several thousand groups are dedicated to cybercrime because of the rewards attached to it (Austin, 2020; Gillespie, 2019; Leukfeldt & Holt, 2019).

It is clearly evident that as people become more dependent on technology, they become easier targets of cybercrime (Hudak, 2019; Martellozzo & Jane, 2017; Steinberg, 2019), as it also could evolve to bring about new problems (Hufnagel & Moiseienko, 2019; Marion & Twede, 2020). It is also important to realize to what extent it is understood by people that either they are really a victim or can be the victim of a cybercrime (Abaimov & Martellini, 2020; Marsh & Melville, 2019).

It is important to realize to what extent cybercrime is understood by people that either they are really a victim or can be the victim of a cybercrime (Azevedo, 2019; Carlson, 2019; Steinberg, 2019). For example, the sending of emails trying to influence people to enter their bank detail is illegal, but almost every one with an email address will have received an email asking them to confirm their bank details (Bancroft, 2019; Bandler & Merzon, 2020).

Another problem is the issue in identifying victims of cybercrime are those situations where people do not know that they have been victimized (Edwards 2019; Graham & Smith, 2019; Hutchings, 2013; Sangster, 2020). Most users of the computer will be aware of the need to install firewall and antivirus software (Littler & Lee, 2020; Schober & Schober; 2019). It is often rare for someone to be told that the program has stopped a virus or potential hack (Kim, 2018; Lavorgna, 2020; Willems, 2019).

It was reported in August 2018 during the Black Hat and Def Con Hacking Conference that, it was possible to even hack patients' vital signs, pacemaker, and insulin pumps in real time (Smith, 2018). According to Symantec (2012), there had been an 81% increase in malicious attacks, i.e. over 5.5 billion attacks. Ponemon Institute, USA (2018) is of the view that 64% of organizations experienced successful endpoint attacks in USA since last year.

The protection against cybercrime largely depends upon the security culture adaptation by government authorities of every networked country, business organizations, and most importantly, every internet user (Abaimov & Martellini, 2020; Sangster, 2020; Steinberg, 2019). Prevention will always be the first and best line of defense along with radical changes in policing and legislation (Gillespie, 2019; Glenny, 2012; Lavorgna, 2020, Willems, 2019). Education and awareness across the citizens will go a long way to prevent individuals against many types of cybercrime and will reduce pertinent risks (Benson, & McAlaney, 2019; Graham & Smith, 2019; Lusthaus, 2012).

Focus of the Chapter

This chapter highlights 11 varieties and skills of cybercrime, focuses on five characteristics, 10 classification, different instruments involved in cybercrime, four aspects regarding cyberterrorism, and seven types of cyber fraud. The impact of cybercrime is also discussed along with cybercrime statistics. Top 10 countries facing cybercrime are also highlighted with international aspects of cybercrime. Initiatives taken by the EU, USA, and China have also been discussed. As cybercrime is a multifaceted problem, therefore, a multidimensional approach is required to understand the subject matter of the respective issue.

The information and data obtained from the literature review related to the research objectives were coded. The coded information was combined under the related topics. After classification and combining, the topics were sorted according to their level of relationship.

Objectives

1. To highlight the varieties and skills of cybercrime along with its characteristics.

2. To discuss the classification and the instruments used in cybercrime.

3. To critically analyze the impact of cybercrime along with cybercrime global statistics.

4. To focus the international aspects of cybercrime and initiatives taken by the EU, USA, and China encompassing cybercrime.

5. To explore the aspects regarding cyberterrorism and the types of cyber fraud.

Research Methodology

This chapter was formed by a systematic review method (Komba & Lwoga, 2020). In this method, the research objectives are determined and an extensive literature review is made on the subject. The findings obtained are classified according to the content of the subject (Petticrew & Roberts, 2006). Classified information is included in the study by organizing it as headings (Pawson et al., 2005). The flow of the study is formed by evaluating classified information and titles (Rahi, 2017). Thus, integrity is ensured by evaluating the researched subject with its contents (Victor, 2008).

Varieties and Skills of Cybercrime

Cybercrime involves various skills and varies greatly, but enlisted aspects have been much stressed upon in the work of scholars like, Bancroft (2019); Johansen (2020); Leukfeldt and Holt (2019); Steinberg (2019); and Troia (2020)

1. Hacking of Computers

2. Denial of Service Attacks (DoS)

3. Distributed Denial of Services Attacks (DDoS)

4. Malware

5. Spyware

6. Offense Relating to Data

7. Destroying, Disclosing, and Accessing Data

8. Misconduct in a Public Office

9. Phishing

10. Pharming

11. Hate and Harm

Characteristics of Cybercrime

According to Marion and Twede (2020); and Steinberg (2019), these are the characteristics of cybercrime in contemporary era.

1. **Scale:** A large number of people are using the internet and related communications, it means that the potential number of victims and offenders is immense.

2. **Accessibility:** The internet continues to reach areas of the world where it has not traditionally been found. This is particularly true in respect of areas where technology is far more widespread

3. **Anonymity:** In most crimes of traditional nature, it is relatively difficult to conceal one's identity. But, it is possible on the internet as it is relatively easy to mask one's identity. So, an average person or investigator can not easily know one's identity.

4. **Portability or Transferability:** With the storage media's rapid growth, it is becoming more difficult to trace its electronic origin. This is particularly true of so-called 'cloud computing', which is often said to involve data being stored in the internet itself. This can

pose significant challenges to investigators who may find that the evidence they require is held outside of their jurisdiction.

5. **Global reach:** The internet as being a global resource poses great challenges with regards to jurisdiction, i.e., whether a country is able to enact its respective laws and whether its investigators have access to such evidences.

Classification of Cybercrime

To understand cybercrime, one should understand it in a broader term, as it is an overarching term that cover a wide range of crimes and behaviors (Benson & McAlaney, 2019; Graham & Smith, 2019; Marion & Twede, 2020). A prominent distinction is to separate 'computer-focused' and 'computer-assisted' crimes (Sangster, 2020). This distinction operates on the very basis that in some cases, computers simply facilitate crime already known to law (Lavorgna, 2020; Marsh & Melville, 2019). Examples of this would be distribution of child pornography and theft. Both of these crimes existed even before the invention of computers and the internet.

However, cyberspace has allowed crimes to be committed in new ways (Abaimov & Martellini, 2020). Phishing (for example) or hacking into the bank account or the publishing of illicit material to a web page. Computer-focused crimes are however different and are those crimes that came into existence because the computer is an essential part of conduct, hacking is an example of it.

Technology advancements have arguably blurred the distinction between computer-assisted and computer-focused crimes (Bandler & Merzon, 2020; Marion & Twede, 2020). It is for the very reason that researchers like Sandywell (2010) suggests the respective encompassing distinctions:

1. Traditional offenses which are generalized as well as radicalized with the help of the internet.

2. Traditional offenses which are enhanced as well as anticipated with the help of the internet.

3. Criminal offenses which are developed with the assistance of the internet.

This provides a useful understanding of cybercrime, i.e., in many cases, there is no new criminal behavior, rather there exists alternate ways of committing old existing behavior. A good example of it would be credit card fraud. As this has existed since its very development (by duplicating receipts, placing 'traps' in ATM machines, etc.). But, with the internet as well as e-commerce growth, it all has led to a new phase of transformation (Lavorgna, 2020; Sangster, 2020).

A secondary example would be bullying. While, bullying has always existed, the use of communication technologies allows the crime to not only flourish, but to develop in a more harmful way (Benson & McAlaney, 2019; Graham & Smith, 2019). A victim could hide from a traditional bully, but it is not easy to escape from a cyberbully (Leukfeldt & Holt, 2019; Willems, 2019; Yar & Steinmetz, 2019). It is simply because of massive use of mobile technologies. We have elaboration on it by a very early writer on cybercrime, i.e. David Wall (2001). He put forward a classification system and he suggested that cybercrime could be categorized as follows:

1. Cyber-violence (hate speech, stalking, etc.)

2. Cyber deceptions and theft (stealing property as well as money)

3. Cyber trespass (the invasion of an individual's cyberspace, hacking, etc.)

4. Cyberpornography (sexual material created or distributed)

Some believe that cybercrime is not a single type of offense and is instead best thought as a broad range of behavior and technologies that are always evolving (Benson & McAlaney, 2019; Graham & Smith, 2019; Leukfeldt & Holt, 2019; Martellozzo & Jane, 2017; Steinberg, 2019; Urbas & Choo, 2008). It is also believed that the most common distinction is between one of three respective categories (Clough, 2010).

1. Crimes in which computer usage is an incidental aspect of the commission of crime, but may afford evidence of it.

2. Existing offenses where the computer is used as a tool to commit any crime (for e.g., child pornography, harassment, etc.).

3. Crimes in which a computer network or a single computer is the target of any criminal activity.

Instruments Used in Cybercrime

It has been noted that the use of technology has transformed over the years and this includes what our understanding regarding a 'computer' (Marion & Twede, 2020). Decades ago, the idea of the computer was a desktop consisting of usually three components, a 'central processing unit', a monitor' and a 'keyboard' (Steinberg, 2019). Laptops do exist lately, but were not as popular today, because they were less powerful and also because battery life was short (Yar & Steinmetz, 2019).

In today's world, the meaning of the computer has changed (Leukfeldt & Holt, 2019; Troia, 2020). While, traditional computers still exist, as do laptops, they are accompanied by a lot of other devices, particularly mobile technologies (Abaimov & Martellini, 2020; Gillespie, 2019). Most smartphones these days have more processing power than NASA would have ever dreamed of when they were initiating their very first space program (Abaimov & Martellini, 2020).

The comparison between a smart phone and computer is highly debated (Graham & Smith, 2019; Leukfeldt & Holt, 2019). While, the functionality may be different, it is most likely that an individual has games on his phone, likely to check email on it, and browse a website. One can send files such as videos, picture, etc. One still refer these devices as the phone, in reality one can consider them as computers. Tablet technology is perhaps even closer to what one thinks as the computer (Bancroft, 2019; Martellozzo & Jane, 2017).

The Convention on Cybercrime (2001) in Budapest, Hungary does provide a definition of the computer system. Article 1(a) defines it as, "any device or a group of interconnected or related devices, one or more of which, pursuit to a program, performs automatic processing of data".

It means that the definition is not based on the physical architecture of the machine, but rather its capabilities. This would also be in accord with the definition commonly used in science which requires automatic storage, retrieval, and processing of information. Because there was some doubt as to whether PDA's, Tablet and Smartphones constitute 'a computer'.

The Cybercrime Convention Committee found it necessary in 2012 to provide the clarification in the context of communication devices, i.e., "The capacity to produce, process and transmit data, such as accessing the internet, sending email, transmitting attachments, upload contents or downloading documents". It supports the assertion that when we consider cybercrime we should consider devices other than traditional computers, but also include all those devices that connect to the internet.

Impact of Cybercrime

According to Norton Cybercrime Report 2011, a cyber security firm, cyber crimes have increased dramatically over the years which cause the sufferings to 431 million victims globally or 14 victims every second. There are around one million cybercrime victims every day. Findings by a research organization, Comparitech, Mr. Paul Bischoff (2018) claims that stock prices are adversely effected by data breaches. In case of a data breach, it can lead to around 0.5 percent decrease in a firm's overall share in market.

A new study, conducted by Bromium and Dr. Michael McGuire, senior lecturer in criminology at the University of Surrey in England, presented at the RSA Conference 2018 in San Francisco has found that the cybercrime economy has grown to $1.5 trillion dollars annually. Cybersecurity Ventures is world's renowned research company with regards to global cyber economy as well as cyber security. In their official annual Cybercrime Report 2017 they predicted that cybercrime will cost the world around $6 trillion annually by 2021.

The escalation of cybercrime is so significant and impacting that cyber law has been a major concern of governments worldwide (Abaimov & Martellini, 2020; Lavorgna, 2020; Littler & Lee, 2020; Marion & Twede, 2020; Marsh & Melville, 2019; Sangster, 2020). Continuous development in cyber law tend to contend more definitive, safe, and uncluttered cyberspace (Austin, 2020; Carlson, 2019; Gillespie, 2019; Hudak, 2019). The development of regulated code of conduct for IT and other electronic medium related to it is an ongoing process to meet the evolving facets of cybercrime (Abaimov & Martellini, 2020; Johansen, 2020; Littler & Lee, 2020; Troia, 2020).

Cybercrime Statistics

According to Alvarez Technology Group (2018); Devon Milkovich (2018); and Patrick Nohe (2018) these are few of the most alarming cybercrime statistics:

1. 95% of breached records came from only three industries worldwide, government, retail, and technology.

2. There is a hacker attack every 39 seconds in US alone according to the study conducted by the Clark School at the University of Maryland, USA.

3. 43% of cyber attacks target small business. 64% of companies have experienced web-based attacks. 62% experienced phishing & social engineering attacks. 59% of companies experienced malicious code and botnets and 51% experienced denial of service attacks.

4. The average cost of a data breach in 2020 will exceed $150 million according to Juniper Research data.

5. Since 2013 there are 3,809,448 records stolen from breaches every day.

6. According to the Q2 2018 Threat Report, Nexusguard's quarterly report, the average distributed denial-of-service (DDoS) attack grew to more than 26Gbps, increasing in size by 500%.

7. Approximately $6 trillion is expected to be spent globally on cyber security by 2021.

8. Unfilled cyber security jobs worldwide will reach $3.5 million by 2021.

9. By 2020 there will be roughly 200 billion connected devices, which means more exposure to cybercrime.

10. 95% of cyber security breaches are due to human error.

11. Only 38% of global organizations claim they are prepared to handle a sophisticated cyber attack.

12. Total cost for cybercrime committed globally has added up to over $1 trillion dollars in 2018.

Top 10 Countries Facing Cybercrime

According to Sumo3000 (2018), following are the top ten countries that are facing cybercrime. These 10 countries face around 63% of the total cybercrime committed across the globe.

1. USA (23%)

2. China (9%)

3. Germany (6%)

4. Britain (5%)

5. Brazil (4%)

6. Spain (4%)

7. Italy (3%)

8. France (3%)

9. Turkey (3%)

10. Poland (3%)

Cyberterrorism

A popular definition of cyberterrorism is the "Intentional use or threat of use, without legally recognized authority, of violence, disruption or interference against cyber system, when it is likely that such use would result in death or injury of a person or persons, substantial damage to physical property, civil order, or significant harm" (Jones, 2005, p.4).

Terrorism is generally seen as an attack against the state's interest, sometimes it even involves attacks against private industry (Lavorgna, 2020; Littler & Lee, 2020). The term itself is easily understood, as it consists of 'cyberspace' and 'terrorism' combination to produce the importance of terrorism that takes place either in, or through the internet. Terrorists have used the internet, specially, from the last decade and this is perhaps a convenient way of reaching a large audience (Bancroft, 2019; Leukfeldt & Holt, 2019; Marsh & Melville, 2019; Martellozzo & Jane, 2017; Willems, 2019; Yar & Steinmetz, 2019).

The main uses of the internet by terrorists according to scholars like Abaimov and Martellini (2020); Austin (2020); Bancroft (2019); Hufnagel and Moiseienko (2019); Jones (2005); Lavorgna (2020); Leukfeldt & Holt (2019); Littler and Lee (2020); Marsh and Melville (2019); Martellozzo and Jane (2017);Willems (2019); Yar and Steinmetz (2019) are:

i. Propaganda

The internet, particularly after the invention of Web 2.0, is a very cheap way to get a message out. The message can also be presented in an uncritical way, something that would not occur through other media. The full extent of this has been seen through the respective videos posted to YouTube which often shows cruel actions of terrorists. Recruitment videos have also been uploaded which present a particularly distorted view of the objectives of the terrorist organization to portray the belief that their activities are in some way just or appropriate.

ii. Fundraising

Terrorism is an expensive business, and yet where it has a political goal that people are sympathetic to, and there will be people who will be prepared to contribute to the cause. It became much easier to have a 'global reach' because a fundraising site can simply be formed and then disseminated through email, social media, as well as hyperlinks.There are a number of online payment systems that would allow people to donate money. The internet also allow anonymous money transfer, which could be particularly attractive in the context of terrorism, as it will allow people to donate money without fearing impacts.

iii. Information Dissemination

This is a little different to propaganda, in it there is dissemination of information that would be useful to the cause, rather than a specific group. The internet has numerous examples of bomb-making instructions and terrorism-aiding manuals. The intention of this dissemination is not necessarily recruitment in a particular group, but rather it is about trying to empower those who are sympathetic to the cause to develop their own strategies for causing terror. Dissemination of such information poses a real risk to society, as it allows people to produce improvised explosive devices cheaply for any cause, potentially widening the likelihood of an attack.

iv. Secure Communication

The internet allows entirely new ways of communicating, for example, VoIP (Voice Over Internet Protocol) software packages such as FaceTime, Facebook,WhatsApp, Skype, etc. An advantage of this is that anonymous email address can be created linked to an anonymous Skype address. Therefore, the chance that authorities being aware of the existence of the call may be remote.

Cyber Fraud

There are other crimes that use technology, i.e., fraud, which is sometimes known as cyber fraud when it is committed online (Benson & McAlaney, 2019; Graham & Smith, 2019; Leukfeldt & Holt, 2019; Yar, 2013). Fraud based behavior exists online as well as offline, but the internet now provides ample opportunities to use it in the form of a new tool (Marion & Twede, 2020; Martellozzo & Jane, 2017; Steinberg, 2019). There is a wide difference regarding the victimhood of fraud (Martellozzo & Jane, 2017; Yar & Steinmetz, 2019). It could possibly range from buying a non-existent item from the internet to MNCs losing millions of dollars annually (Sandwell, 2010; Sangster, 2020; Schober & Schober, 2019).

a) Variety of Frauds

There is a variety of frauds committed on the internet. Indeed, new forms are also developing each year (Azevedo, 2018; Benson & McAlaney, 2019; Hufnagel & Moiseienko, 2019; Lavorgna, 2020). A closer analysis of fraud suggests that there are seven types.

i. **Fraud through low-level trickery:** This includes scam as advertising non-existent or bogus item for sale.

ii. **Fraud through developed story-based application:** This is where a relationship is developed between the scammer and victim.

iii. **Participation through employment-based strategies:** This could include the advertisement of a job that requires the completion of course or application that involves an advance fee.

iv. **Fraud through implied necessary obligation:** This type of scams require the user's response before the scam actually works. It could include unintentional subscription to a particular website that requires the user to call a particular number, so they can be charged for it.

v. **Information gathering through apparently authentic appeals:** This would include the scam of spoofing as well as phishing.

vi. **Financial gain through merchant and customer based exploitation:** Mostly, it includes internet auction fraud.

vii. **Financial gain through marketing opportunities:** This would include charity fraud as well as ponzi schemes, which of course, turn out to be false.

(b) **Romance Fraud**

There has been a resurgence in recent years where people have been targeted through romance websites (Graham & Smith, 2019; Martellozzo & Jane, 2017). In recent years, one of the biggest growth areas on the world wide web are dating portals (Benson & McAlaney, 2019). The desire of people to communicate with each other in a romantic manner allows people to be defrauded (Hudak, 2019; Leukfeldt & Holt, 2019). There are thousands of complaints concerning romance fraud with losses over millions of dollars annually worldwide (Gillespie, 2019; Steinberg, 2019; Yar & Steinmetz, 2019).

International Aspects of Cybercrime

The significance of respective issues made developing countries more concerned to cautiously build and deploy the security and trust (Abaimov & Martellini, 2020; Austin, 2020; Lavorgna, 2020; Littler & Lee, 2020). So, the benefits and advantages of ICTs can serve their citizen not only for commercial activities, but its application can be make useful at societal level such as health, education, and e-government, etc. (Bancroft, 2019; Carlson, 2019; Gillespie, 2019).

According to Hufnagel and Moiseienko (2019); Lavorgna (2020); Marsh and Melville (2019); Schober and Schober (2019) the international aspects of cyber laws encompasses:

1. To identify cybercrime threats and vulnerabilities and deploy solutions to secure ICT infrastructure for internet consumers and its application on different networks using pertinent technologies.

2. To support and work along with member states in gradual developments of laws and set exemplary legislation for internet services, internet security, its ethical issues, deterrence of cybercrime, data security, as well as privacy.

3. To increase security and make cyber environment as unattractive as possible to cyber criminal, so that confidence of consumer is enhance while using internet services and respective applications.

4. To develop hardware and software tools to promote and exchange best possible practices on ICTs security and related legitimate concerns in the respective areas.

Initiatives by the EU and USA

The initiatives regarding cyber law by the United States of America are discussed below because of the role of USA as a global superpower in terms of technology and world's strongest economy in terms of nominal GDP, i.e. $21.43 trillion. While, the European Union is a political and economic union of 28 member states, and accounts for being the strongest monetary union in the world with a nominal GDP $18.70 trillion. People's Republic of China is the third largest economy of the world after the US and the EU. It boosts for being a regional superpower as it has a nominal GDP of $14.14 trillion (IMF, 2020).

The foremost federal law enforcement agencies which are responsible for investigation of cybercrime at domestic level include:

1. United States Secret Service (USSS)

2. Federal Bureau of Investigation (FBI)

3. United States Postal Inspection Service (USPIS)

4. United States Immigration and Customs Enforcement (ICE)

5. Bureau of Alcohol, Tobacco and Firearms (ATF)

USA's experience and knowledge in the field of legislation regarding cyber security is significant. The USA has organized and featured structure for consumers of ICT to report cybercrime against them.

1. Every state has offices for cybercrime monitoring agencies where crime can be reported conveniently. Every state office has a predefined contact information which is easy to access and cybercrime can be reported to the local office of concerned agency by even a phone call to an available duty complaint officer.

2. Every law enforcement agency headquarters are situated in Washington, D.C, where a number of law enforcing officers who are well trained and specialized in their particular fields are working vigilantly. Federal Bureau of Investigation and USA Secret Service, both have their head offices in Washington and are responsible for protecting forcible intrusion by cyber criminals. For most of the time, the aim of cyber criminals is either monetary gains or access to classified data. Generally, they are termed as hackers, i.e., they hack into legitimate computer networks.

3. Federal Bureau of Investigation in collaboration with National White Crime Complaint Centre, another US prominent agency, established Internet Crime Complaint Centre (IC3) in 2000. It is serving as a platform to receive cybercrime complaints, develop strategies, and refer cybercrime complaints to confront increasing cyber threats.

4. The IC3 has remarkably a positive staff culture regarding cybercrime victims where one can report crime because of their friendly reporting system which immediately make sure that concerned authorities are notified and appropriate action against cyber criminal has been initiated. IC3 also makes sure that the central referral mechanism is intact for regulatory and law enforcement agencies at the federal, state, and local level.

While, in almost all European Union countries, the European Union has implemented more or less the same rules as implemented in the USA regarding regulations on electronic trade and commerce through legislation and even makes sure that non-member countries align their laws with the EU initiative before formally joining it (Fuster & Jasmontaite, 2020; Jones, 2005; Synodinou et al., 2020; Summers et al., 2014).

Initiatives by China

The second largest internet users after USA are from the People's Republic of China. There are approximately 111 million internet users in this country. China reaps the advantages of technological growth, but at the same time while such a huge number of people were accessing internet, regulation as well as supervision from authorities were lacking. It caused a rampant growth in cybercrime, which include the spread of pornographic material, hate and harm content, illicit gambling, online frauds, etc. Chinese authorities addressed the issues exemplary. They deployed surveillance and regulated their internet users, which not only mitigated the growth of cybercrime, but also left a positive growth on their e-trade.

Shenzhen, in southeastern China, is a modern metropolis, according to the statistics presented by the Shenzhen Association of Online Media and the China Internet Network Information Center (CINIC), there were 8.97 million internet users in Shenzhen by the end of 2015. The highest ratio nationwide, which is 83.2 percent of Shenzhen's total population, is on top of achieving success regarding online crimes and rapid spread of malicious and hazardous information by forming a cyber police force.

Cyber police in China has developed a system to patrol and keep active presence on online activities of users. When a user gets online, an icon which shows the presence of police department flashes on the user's screen. Whenever a user needs to contact for a cybercrime complain, he just has to click the respective icon, and can report to the immediate complaint officer in few minutes.

In a few months time, cyber police has been notified regarding online crimes by clicking icon that accumulated around 100,000 clicks, which include more that 600 consultation services on cybercrime legislation along with 1,600 reports of online criminal activities, out of which 235 have been forwarded for legal proceedings. The Ministry of Public Security has decided to establish cyber police in eight major cities of China after the success in Shenzhen.

Solutions and Recommendations

1. General public awareness programs should be initiated with regards to cybercrime. It can be done via engaging community as well as CBOs, NGOs, INGOs, and cyber vigilantism.

2. During the process of legislation regarding cybercrime expert opinion should be included, like criminologists, psychologists, sociologists, IT professionals, etc.

3. Students should be educate regarding the vulnerabilities of cyber world via seminars and workshops.

4. A strong global cyber force is required who can counter cyber threats.

5. At domestic level, special task force (i.e. cyber police) should be developed to especially ensure online routine checks at the facilities where public internet access is available.

6. Proper cybercrime data should be maintained by respective countries and it should be shared to the possible extent.

7. Scholars should discuss cybercrime issue on different forums, specially in print as well as electronic media.

8. Criminological courses focusing on cybercrime should also be included in the regular studies of IT, social science education, law studies, business studies, etc.

9. Victims of cybercrime are large in number, there should be easy access of the victims where they can complain regarding e-offenses.

10. The respective legal departments should be equipped with the latest investigating technologies.

11. To effectively deal with the cases of cybercrime, the respective judiciary (especially in the undeveloped countries) should be given proper training.

Additional Solutions (for individuals):

12. Use your own computer and terminate online sessions completely.

13. Use security programs, protect your passwords, and visit only trustworthy websites.

14. Use privacy settings to prevent personal information being broadcast via social networking.

15. Clear all your history after logging off your account and update your software package regularly.

16. Do not open any links in emails from strangers.

17. Encryption of file and regular backups of significant data is very important.

18. Limiting the administrative powers of all accounts in case of a shared devices.

19. Unknown Wi-Fi networks and Bluetooth connections should be avoided.

20. E-transactions must be entered via websites that are authentic, and data should not be saved on online servers.

Future Research Directions

Significant areas for conducting future research encompassing cybercrime via engaging qualitative, qualitative, or eclectic approach can be:

1. Computer-focused as well as computer-assisted crimes

2. Criminal psychology

3. Cyberterrorism

4. Cyber security

5. Perceived and actual risks

Conclusion

Research studies into cybercrime are nominal as the field is relatively new. The internet is possibly today's most compelling innovative invention, as it proceeds to change everyday life of an individual who uses it. But, on the contrary, the advancement of technology will certainly lead to a transformation of cybercrime, which is why, some prefer to think of cybercrime as an ever changing set of behavior. Cybercrime, the offspring of contemporary technology could only be controlled and prevented by means of strong strong cyber legislation as well as concrete initiatives. Nations worldwide are facing the perils of cybercrime because of numerous reasons, e.g., poor technology, absence as well as the incapacity of legislation regarding financial constraints, and lack of cooperation with international law enforcing agencies.

References

Abaimov, S., & Martellini, M. (2020). *Cyber arms security in cyberspace.* Boca Raton, CRC Press. ISBN: 9780367853860

Alvarez Technology Group (2018). *2018 top cybercrime facts and why you should care.* https://www.alvareztg.com/2018-cybercrime-statistics-reference-material/

Austin, G. (2020). *National cyber emergencies: The return to civil defence.* London, Routledge. ISBN: 9780367360344

Azevedo, F. U. B. (2018). *Hackers exposed: Discover the secret world of cybercrime.* Independently published. ISBN-13: 978-1718124615

Bancroft, A. (2019). *The darknet and smarter crime: Methods for Investigating criminal entrepreneurs and the illicit drug economy (Palgrave studies in cybercrime and cybersecurity).* Cham, Palgrave Macmillan. ISBN-13: 978-3030265113

Bandler, J., & Merzon, A. (2020). *Cybercrime investigations: A comprehensive resource for everyone.* Boca Raton, CRC Press. ISBN-13:978-0367196233

Benson, V., & McAlaney, J. (2019). *Emerging cyber threats and cognitive vulnerabilities* (1st ed.). Academic Press. ISBN-13: 978-0128162033

Bischoff, P. (2018, September 6). *Analysis: How data breaches affect stock market share prices.* https://www.comparitech.com/blog/information-security/data-breach-share-price- 2018/

Black Hat and Def Con Hacking Conference. (August - 2018). https://www.blackhat.com/us-18/defcon.html

Bromium, & McGuire, M. (2018, April). *RSA Conference 2018.* San Francisco, USA. https://www.rsaconference.com/events/us18

Carlson, C. T. (2019). *How to manage cybersecurity risk: A security leader's roadmap with open fair.* Universal Publishers. ISBN-13: 978-1627342766

Clough, J. (2011). *Principles of cybercrime.* NY: Cambridge University Press.

Convention on Cybercrime. (2001). European Treaty Series - No. 185. https://rm.coe.int/1680081561

Cybercrime. (2020). In *Collins English Dictionary.* https://www.collinsdictionary.com/dictionary/english/cybercrime

Cybercrime. (2020). In *Encyclopedia Britannica.* https://www.britannica.com/topic/cybercrime

Cybercrime. (2020). In *Merriam-Webster.* https://www.merriam-webster.com/dictionary/cybercrime

Cybercrime. (2020). In *Oxford Advanced Learner's Dictionary.* https://www.oxfordlearnersdictionaries.com/definition/english/cybercrime

Cybercrime. (2020). In *The Chambers Dictionary.* https://www.cybercrimechambers.com/blog-web-jacking-117.php

Cybercrime Convention Committee Proceedings. (2012). https://www.coe.int/en/web/cybercrime/tcy

Cybersecurity Ventures. Cybercrime Report, 2017. https://cybersecurityventures.com/hackerpocalypse-cybercrime-report-2016/

Edwards, G. (2019). *Cybercrime investigators* (1st ed.). Hoboken, Wiley. ISBN-13: 978-1119596288

Fuster, G. G., Jasmontaite, L. (2020). Cybersecurity regulation in the European Union: The digital, the critical and fundamental rights. In Christen, M., Gordijn, B., Loi, M. (eds). *The Ethics of Cybersecurity. The* International Library of Ethics, Law and Technology, (21). Cham: Springer. doi: https://doi.org/10.1007/978-3-030-29053-5_5

Gillespie, A. A. (2019). *Cybercrime: Key issues and debates*, London, Routledge. ISBN: 9781351010283

Glenny, M. (2012). *DarkMarket: How hackers became the new media.* NY: Vintage Books.

Graham, R. S., & Smith, S. K. (2019). *Cybercrime and digital deviance* (1st ed.). New York, Routledge. ISBN: 9780815376316

Hudak, H. C. (2019). *Cybercrime (Privacy in the digital age).* North Star Editions. ISBN-13: 978-1644940815

Hufnagel, S., & Moiseienko, A. (2019). *Criminal networks and law enforcement: Global perspectives on illegal enterprise.* London, Routledge.

Hutchings, A. (2013). *Theory and crime: Does it compute?.* Australia: Griffith University.

International Monetary Fund (2020). *World economic outlook database.* https://www.imf.org/external/pubs/ft/weo/2019/02/weodata/index.aspx

Johansen, G. (2020). *Digital forensics and incident response: Incident response techniques and procedures to respond to modern cyber threats.* Birmingham, Packt Publishing. ISBN-13: 978-1838649005

Jones, C. W. (2005, April). *Council of Europe convention on cybercrime: Themes and critiques.* Workshop on the international dimensions of cyber security. Hosted by Georgia Institute of Technology and Carnegie Mellon University, USA.

Kim, P. (2018). *The hacker playbook 3: Practical guide to penetration testing.* Independently published. ISBN-13: 978-1980901754

Komba, M. M., & Lwoga, E. T. (2020). *Systematic review as a research method in library and information science.* DOI: 10.4018/978-1-7998-1471-9.ch005.

Lavorgna, A. (2020). *Cybercrimes: Critical issues in a global context.* Springer. ISBN-13: 978-1352009118

Leukfeldt, R., & Holt, T. J. (2019). *The human factor of cybercrime.* London, Routledge. ISBN-13: 978-1138624696

Littler, M., & Lee, B. (2020). *Digital extremisms: Readings in violence, radicalisation and extremism in the online space.* Cham, Springer Nature Switzerland AG. ISBN13: 9783030301378

Lusthaus, J. (2012). Trust in the world of cybercrime. *Global Crime, 13*(2), 71-94.

Marion, N. E., & Twede, J. (2020). *Cybercrime: An encyclopedia of digital crime.* Santa Barbara, ABC-CLIO. ISBN-13: 978-1440857348

Marsh, B., & Melville, G. (2019). *Crime, justice and the media.* London, Routledge. ISBN: 9780429432194

Martellozzo, E., & Jane, E. A. (2017). *Cybercrime and its victims.* London, Routledge.

Milkovich, D. (2018, December 3). *13 alarming cyber security facts and stats.*
https://www.cybintsolutions.com/cyber-security-facts-stats/

Nohe, P. (2018, September 27). *Re-hashed: 2018 cybercrime statistics: A closer look at the web of profit".* https://www.thesslstore.com/blog/2018-cybercrime- statistics/

Norton Cybercrime Report (2011).
http://us.norton.com/content/en/us/home_homeoffice/html/cybercrimereport/

Pawson, R., Greenhalgh, T., Harvey, G, & Walshe, K. (2005). Realist review - A new method of systematic review designed for complex policy interventions. *Journal of Health Services Research & Policy, 10*(1), 21-34.

Petticrew, M., & Roberts, H. (2006). *Systematic reviews in the social sciences: A   practical guide.* DOI: 10.1002/9780470754887

Ponemon   Institute.   (2018).   *State   of   endpoint   security   risk.*
https://www.businesswire.com/news/home/20181016005758/en/Study-Reveals64-Organiza tions-Experienced-Successful-Endpoint

Rahi, S. (2017). Research design and methods: A systematic review of research paradigms, sampling issues and instruments development. *International Journal of Economics & Management Sciences, (6).* DOI: 10.4172/2162-6359.1000403.

Sandwell, B. (2010). On the globalisation of crime: The internet and new criminality. In Y. Jewkes & M. Yar, *Handbook of internet crime* (pp. 38-66). Uffculme, England: Willan Publishing.

Sangster, M. (2020). *No safe harbor: The inside truth about cybercrime-and how to protect your business.* Vancouver, Page Two. ISBN-13: 978-1989603420

Schober, S. N., & Schober, C. W. (2019). *Cybersecurity is everybody's business: Solve the security puzzle for your small business and home.* ScottSchober.com Publishing.   ISBN-13: 978-0996902267

Shenzhen Association of Online Media and China Internet Network Information Center (2015). http://english.sz.gov.cn/ln/201601/t20160121_3452230.htm

Smith. (2018). *Hacking pacemakers, insulin pumps and patients' vital signs in real time.* https://www.csoonline.com/article/3296633/security/hacking-pacemakers-insulin- pumps-and-patients-vital-signs-in-real-time.html

Steinberg, J. (2019). *Cybersecurity for dummies (For dummies computer/tech).* Hoboken, John Wiley & Sons. ISBN: 9781119560326

Summers, S. J., Schwarzenegger, C., Ege, G., Young, F., & Bohlander, M. (2014). *The emergence of EU criminal law: Cyber crime and the regulation of the information society (Studies in international and comparative criminal law).* ISBN-13 : 978-1841137278

Summo3000 (2018). *Top 20 countries found to have the most cybercrime.* https://www.enigmasoftware.com/top-20-countries-the-most-cybercrime/

Symantec White Paper - Turning the Tables on Malware. (2012). https://www.symantec.com/content/en/us/enterprise/white_papers/b-turning_the_tables_on_ malware_WP_21155056.en-us.pdf

Synodinou, T. E., Jougleux, P., Markou, C., & Prastitou-Merdi, T. (Eds.). (2020). *EU internet law in the digital era - Regulation and enforcement.* Springer International Publishing. doi: 10.1007/978-3-030-25579-4

Troia, V. (2020). *Hunting cyber criminals: A hacker's guide to online Intelligence gathering tools and techniques.* Indianapolis, Wiley. ISBN-13: 978-1119540922

Urbas, G., & Choo, K. R. (2008). *Resource materials on technology-enabled crime.* Canberra, Australia: Australian Institute of Criminology. ISBN: 9781921185700.

Victor, L. (2008) Systematic reviewing in the social sciences: Outcomes and explanation . *Enquire 1(1),* 32-46.

Wall, D. S. (Ed.). (2001). *Crime and the internet.* NY: Routledge.

Willems, E. (2019). *Cyberdanger: Understanding and guarding against cybercrime.* Springer International Publishing. ISBN:978-3-030-04531-9

Yar, M. (2013). *Cybercrime and society.* London: Sage Publishing Ltd.

Yar, M., & Steinmetz, K. F. (2019). *Cybercrime and society* (3rd ed.). SAGE Publications Ltd. ISBN-13: 978-1526440648

Additional Readings

1. Beaver, K. (2017). *Hacking for dummies* (5th ed). ISBN-13: 978-1119154686

2. Moore, R. (2005). Cybercrime: Investigating high technology computer crime. NY: Matthew Bender & Company. ISBN 1-59345-303-5.

3. Nair, A. (2018). *The regulation of internet pornography: Issues and challenges.* UK: Routledge.

4. Ogilvie, E. (2000). Cyberstalking. *Trends and Issues in Crime and Criminal Justice,* 166.

5. Sternberg, J. (2012). *Misbehavior in cyber places: The regulation of online conduct in virtual communities on the internet.* MD: Rowman & Littlefield.

6. Wall, D. (2007). *Cybercrime: The transformation of crime in the information age.* Cambridge: Polity Books.

7. Wall, D. S., (Ed.). (2001). *Crime and the internet.* NY: Routledge.

8. Webber, C. (2014). *Hackers and cybercrime. Shades of deviance: A primer on crime, deviance and social harm.* London: Routledge.

9. Yar, M. (2013). *Cybercrime and society.* London: Sage Publishing Ltd.

10. Zhang, X., Tsang, A., Yue, W. T., & Chau, M. (2015). The classification of hackers by knowledge exchange behaviors. *Information Systems Frontiers,* 1-13.

Key Terms

1. **Accessibility:** The quality of being able to be reached.

2. **Anonymity:** The condition of being unknown.

3. **Computer-assisted crimes:** Crimes in which a computer or computers are used for another criminal offense.

4. **Computer-focused crimes:** Crimes in which a computer or computers are targeted.

5. **Cybercrime:** The use of a computer to commit a crime.

6. **Global reach:** The ability to reach worldwide.

7. **Portability:** The ability to be easily carried.

Chapter 3: Legislation of Cybercrime in Pakistan

Abstract

Research studies into cybercrime with regards to the Pakistani context are nominal, as the field is relatively new. Pakistani has a perfect ecosystem regarding cybercrime, as the internet is widely available. The problem in identifying victims of cybercrime in Pakistan are those situations where people do not know that they have been victimized. Cyber laws in Pakistan are in their initial phase and much efforts are required to ensure the protection of people from cybercrime in the Pakistani context. Most common types of cybercrime in Pakistan and the South Asian region are criminal access, e-fraud and e-forgery, misuse of devices and encryption, cyberstalking, pornography, malicious code, spamming, unauthorized interception, cyberterrorism, attempt and aiding or abetting. But, relationship fraud is the most serious and heinous in terms of its nature. Unfortunately, it is one of the most prevalent types of cybercrime in Pakistan as social media usage is increasing exponentially. The internet is widely available and offers an opportunity to meet people from opposite gender, which was impossible in previous times. Unfortunately, Pakistan possess a quintessential environment for the growth of cybercrime. A few women in Pakistan have awareness regarding the dangers of sharing online information. Social mores in Pakistan always hold women responsible, if something goes wrong. This chapter delves into Pakistani laws encompassing cybercrime that exist to control or mitigate the respective critical issue. This chapter will elaborate the strength and weakness of Pakistani cybercrime laws and explore the vulnerable areas for criminal for the cyber offense.

Keywords: cybercrime, cybercrime legislation, cyberstalking, cyberterrorism, cyber world, cyber security, Pakistan.

Introduction

Cybercrime has so advanced that it was reported in August 2018 during the Black Hat and Def Con Hacking Conference that, it was possible to even hack patients' vital signs, pacemaker, and insulin pumps in real time (Smith, 2018). A Barkly sponsored survey of 660 IT companies and professionals by Ponemon Institute, USA (2018) 'State of Endpoint Security Risk' has revealed that 64% of organizations experienced successful endpoint attacks.

Cybercrime's pace globally is on a high rise (Johansen, 2020; Troia, 2020). It is an offense that is even harder to identify and resolve as compared to traditional crimes (Gillespie, 2019). Cybercrime cells all around the world receives thousands of complaints on a daily basis (Martellozzo & Jane, 2017). Cybercriminals are honing their skills, while consumers remain unconcerned (Marion & Twede, 2020). Cybercriminals are innovative, organized, and far sophisticated (Hutchings, 2013; Marsh & Melville, 2019).

The protection against cybercrime largely depends upon the security culture adaptation by government authorities of every networked country, business organizations, and most importantly, every internet user (Benson & McAlaney, 2019; Yar & Steinmetz, 2019). Prevention will always be the first and best line of defense along with radical changes in policing and legislation (Austin, 2020; Glenny, 2012; Leukfeldt & Holt, 2019). Education and awareness across the citizens will go a long way to prevent individuals against many types of cybercrime and will reduce pertinent risks (Hudak, 2019; Lusthaus, 2012; Steinberg, 2019).

Cybercrime can be defined in multiple ways; in the broadest sense, any offense involving a computer system may be included in this category. Few definitions encompassing the subject matter are cited.

According to Merriam-Webster (2020), "Criminal activity (such as fraud, theft, or distribution of child pornography) committed using a computer especially to illegally access, transmit, or manipulate data". While, in accordance with Oxford Advanced Learner's Dictionary (2020), "Crime that is committed using the internet, for example by stealing somebody's personal or bank details or by infecting their computer with a virus".

"Cybercrime is a crime committed by means of computers or the internet" (Collins English Dictionary, 2020). While according to The Chambers Dictionary (2020), "Criminal activity or a crime that involves the internet, a computer system, or computer technology".

Encyclopedia Britannica (2020) states, "Cybercrime, the use of a computer as an instrument to further illegal ends, such as committing fraud, trafficking in child pornography and intellectual property, stealing identities, or violating privacy. Cybercrime, especially through the Internet, has grown in importance as the computer has".

The Government of Pakistan passed the Electronic Transaction Ordinance in 2002. It was aimed at recognizing as well as facilitating e-transactions, records, communications, documents, information, and providing for certification service provider's accreditation. The respective framework, i.e., ETO 2002 has provided Pakistan with an initial legal backing regarding e-information as well as communication.

National Response Centre for Cyber Crime (NR3C) formed in 2007 is another initiative taken by the Government of Pakistan to trace cybercriminals and to counter the internet misuse.

While, the National Assembly of Pakistan has passed the draft of Prevention of Electronic Crimes Act, 2016 (PECA) on 13th April, 2016. This is promulgated by the government as being the latest development to curb the issue of cybercrime in Pakistan.

Although, the PECA has been approved and came into system, but there is huge criticism from the opposition and the IT industry. Critics believe it to be harsh, with punishments not fitting the respective crimes. Another problem is the bill's language, as it could be abused by the government as well as law enforcement agencies in Pakistan.

Focus of the Chapter

This chapter focuses on the cybercrime situation in Pakistan, role of Pakistan in the cyberworld, Electronic Transactions Ordinance (2002), role of National Response Centre for Cyber Crime, cybercrime legislation in Pakistan, as well as the role of Prevention of Electronic Crimes Act (2016).

Objectives

1.   To examine the cybercrime situation in Pakistan.

2.   To discuss the role of Pakistan in the cyberworld.

3.   To discuss the Electronic Transactions Ordinance, 2002.

4.   To discuss the role of National Response Centre for Cyber Crime.

5.   To elaborate the legislation of cyber laws in Pakistan.

6.   To critically analyze the role of Prevention of Electronic Crimes Act, 2016.

Research Methodology

This chapter was formed by a systematic review method (Komba & Lwoga, 2020). In this method, the research objectives are determined and an extensive literature review is made on the subject. The findings obtained are classified according to the content of the subject (Petticrew & Roberts, 2006). Classified information is included in the study by organizing it as headings (Pawson et al., 2005). The flow of the study is formed by evaluating classified information and titles (Rahi, 2017). Thus, integrity is ensured by evaluating the researched subject with its contents (Victor, 2008).

As a result, this method was adopted and these procedures were followed respectively. The information and data obtained from the literature review related to the research objectives were coded. The coded information was combined under the related topics. After classification and combining, the topics were sorted according to their level of relationship.

Significance of Cyber Laws

Yoshio Utsumi was the former Secretary General of International Telecommunication Union (ITU) from 1998 to 2006. ITU is a specialized agency of the United Nations. It is responsible for issues that concern Information and Communication Technologies. He accentuated the significance of immediate measures for security of cyberspace, Information and Communication Technology Systems (ICTs), and its infrastructure.

Findings by a research organization, Comparitech, Mr. Paul Bischoff (2018) claims that stock prices are adversely effected by data breaches. In case of a data breach, it can lead to around 0.5 percent decrease in a firm's overall share in market.

A new study, conducted by Bromium and Dr. Michael McGuire, senior lecturer in criminology at the University of Surrey in England, presented at the RSA Conference 2018 in San Francisco has found that the cybercrime economy has grown to $1.5 trillion dollars annually. Cybersecurity Ventures is world's renowned research company with regards to global cyber economy as well as cyber security. In their official annual Cybercrime Report 2017 they predicted that cybercrime will cost the world around $6 trillion annually by 2021.

The escalation of cybercrime is so significant and impacting that cyber law has been a major concern of governments worldwide (Hufnagel & Moiseienko, 2019). Continuous development in cyber law tend to contend more definitive, safe, and uncluttered cyberspace (Austin, 2020). The development of regulated code of conduct for IT and other electronic medium related to it is an ongoing process to meet the evolving facets of cybercrime (Johansen, 2020; Marion & Twede, 2020; Troia, 2020).

Cybercrime Statistics

According to Alvarez Technology Group (2018); Devon Milkovich (2018); and Patrick Nohe (2018) these are few of the most alarming cybercrime statistics:

1. 95% of breached records came from only three industries worldwide, government, retail, and technology.

2. There is a hacker attack every 39 seconds in US alone according to the study conducted by the Clark School at the University of Maryland, USA.

3. 43% of cyber attacks target small business. 64% of companies have experienced web-based attacks. 62% experienced phishing & social engineering attacks. 59% of companies experienced malicious code and botnets and 51% experienced denial of service attacks.

4. The average cost of a data breach in 2020 will exceed $150 million according to Juniper Research data.

5. Since 2013 there are 3,809,448 records stolen from breaches every day.

6. According to the Q2 2018 Threat Report, Nexusguard's quarterly report, the average distributed denial-of-service (DDoS) attack grew to more than 26Gbps, increasing in size by 500%.

7. Approximately $6 trillion is expected to be spent globally on cyber security by 2021.

8. Unfilled cyber security jobs worldwide will reach $3.5 million by 2021.

9. By 2020 there will be roughly 200 billion connected devices, which means more exposure to cybercrime.

10. 95% of cyber security breaches are due to human error.

11. Only 38% of global organizations claim they are prepared to handle a sophisticated cyber attack.

12. Total cost for cybercrime committed globally has added up to over $1 trillion dollars in 2018.

Top 10 Countries Facing Cybercrime

According to Sumo3000, Enigma Software Group, USA (2018), following are the top ten countries that are facing cybercrime. These 10 countries face around 63% of the total cybercrime committed across the globe.

1. USA (23%)

2. China (9%)

3. Germany (6%)

4. Britain (5%)

5. Brazil (4%)

6. Spain (4%)

7. Italy (3%)

8. France (3%)

9. Turkey (3%)

10. Poland (3%)

Initiatives by the EU and USA

The initiatives regarding cyber law by the United States of America are discussed below because of the role of USA as a global superpower in terms of technology and world's strongest economy in terms of nominal GDP, i.e. $21.43 trillion. While, the European Union is a political and economic union of 28 member states, and accounts for being the strongest monetary union in the world with a nominal GDP $18.70 trillion. People's Republic of China is the third largest economy of the world after the US and the EU. It boosts for being a regional superpower as it has a nominal GDP of $14.14 trillion (IMF, 2020).

USA's experience and knowledge in the field of legislation regarding cyber security is significant. The USA has organized and featured structure for consumers of ICT to report cybercrime against them. The foremost federal law enforcement agencies which are responsible for investigation of cybercrime at domestic level include:

1. United States Secret Service (USSS)

2. Federal Bureau of Investigation (FBI)

3. United States Postal Inspection Service (USPIS)

4. United States Immigration and Customs Enforcement (ICE)

5. Bureau of Alcohol, Tobacco and Firearms (ATF)

Every state has offices for cybercrime monitoring agencies where crime can be reported conveniently. Every state office has a predefined contact information which is easy to access and cybercrime can be reported to the local office of concerned agency by even a phone call to an available duty complaint officer. Every law enforcement agency headquarters are situated in Washington, D.C, where a number of law enforcing officers who are well trained and specialized in their particular fields are working vigilantly. Federal Bureau of Investigation and USA Secret Service, both have their head offices in Washington and are responsible for protecting forcible intrusion by cybercriminals. For most of the time, the aim of cybercriminals is either monetary gains or access to classified data. Generally, they are termed as hackers, i.e., they hack into legitimate computer networks.

Federal Bureau of Investigation in collaboration with National White Crime Complaint Centre, another US prominent agency, established Internet Crime Complaint Centre (IC3) in 2000. It is serving as a platform to receive cybercrime complaints, develop strategies, and refer cybercrime complaints to confront increasing cyber threats.

The IC3 has remarkably a positive staff culture regarding cybercrime victims where one can report crime because of their friendly reporting system which immediately make sure that concerned authorities are notified and appropriate action against cyber criminal has been initiated. IC3 also makes sure that the central referral mechanism is intact for regulatory and law enforcement agencies at the federal, state, and local level.

Other Initiatives by the Government of United States regarding Cybercrime:

1. Online Copyright Infringement Liability Limitation Act - 1998

2. Digital Millennium Copyright Act - 1998

3. Uniform Computer Information Transactions Act - 1999

4. Internet Fraud Complaint Center (IFCC)   (founded in 2000)

5. U.S. Computer Emergency Readiness Team (founded in 2003)

6. Controlling the Assault of Non-Solicited Pornography And Marketing Act - 2003

7. Proposed EU Directives on the patentability of computer-implemented inventions.

8. National Association of Attorney General's Computer Crime Point of Contact List.

9. Department of Homeland Security's National Infrastructure Coordinating Center.

While, in almost all European Union countries, the European Union has implemented more or less the same rules as implemented in the USA regarding regulations on electronic trade and commerce through legislation and even makes sure that non-member countries align their laws with the EU initiative before formally joining it (Fuster & Jasmontaite, 2020; Jones, 2005; Synodinou et al., 2020; Summers et al., 2014).

Initiatives by China

The second largest internet users after USA are from the People's Republic of China. There are approximately 111 million internet users in this country. China reaps the advantages of technological growth, but at the same time while such a huge number of people were accessing internet, regulation as well as supervision from authorities were lacking. It caused a rampant growth in cybercrime, which include the spread of pornographic material, hate and harm content, illicit gambling, online frauds, etc. Chinese authorities addressed the issues exemplary. They deployed surveillance and regulated their internet users, which not only mitigated the growth of cybercrime, but also left a positive growth on their e-trade.

Shenzhen, in southeastern China, is a modern metropolis, according to the statistics presented by the Shenzhen Association of Online Media and the China Internet Network Information Center (CINIC), there were 8.97 million internet users in Shenzhen by the end of 2015. The highest ratio nationwide, which is 83.2 percent of Shenzhen's total population, is on top of achieving success regarding online crimes and rapid spread of malicious and hazardous information by forming a cyber police force.

Cyber police in China has developed a system to patrol and keep active presence on online activities of users. When a user gets online, an icon which shows the presence of police department flashes on the user's screen. Whenever a user needs to contact for a cybercrime complain, he just has to click the respective icon, and can report to the immediate complaint officer in few minutes.

In a few months time, cyber police has been notified regarding online crimes by clicking icon that accumulated around 100,000 clicks, which include more that 600 consultation services on cybercrime legislation along with 1,600 reports of online criminal activities, out of which 235 have been forwarded for legal proceedings. The Ministry of Public Security has decided to establish cyber police in eight major cities of China after the success in Shenzhen.

Cybercrime Situation in Pakistan

According to a 2017 report by Bytes for All, Pakistan (digital rights organization), more than 30 million of Pakistan's 212 million people use the internet via mobile devices. The pace of cybercrime growth within Pakistan is increasing dramatically. It is a swift emerging felony which is even hard to identify. The cybercrime cell in Pakistan receives around 12 complaints on a daily basis. In order to resolve these crimes, stern initiatives have to be ensured, so that individuals feel protected while surfing the internet.

Role of Pakistan in the Cyberworld

The Islamic Republic of Pakistan is a sovereign state located in South Asia. According to Bureau of Statistics - 6th Population and Housing Census, Pakistan's population is 212,742,631. It is the fifth most populous country and the second most populous Muslim country in the world after Indonesia. According to Internet World Stats (IWS), in Pakistan, total number of internet users in October 2018 were 44,608,065, which is 22.2% of the total population.

The internet in Pakistan is available since early 1990s and the IT industry is one of the largest and fastest growing industry. Use of internet by individuals for online trade, education, social media, communication, etc. is very common. Even government services apps are facilitating people, like National Database and Registration Authority, Pakistan (NADRA), Federal Board of Revenue (FBR), etc.

The misuse of technology is also very common in Pakistan, as the rate of cybercrime is increasing rapidly. Pakistan is also among the countries which are facing transnational cybercriminals along with internal threats. Pakistan has also addressed the cybercrime situation seriously and developed a legal framework. Electronic Transactions Ordinance which was passed in 2002, ensures the security of documents, information, records, communication and transactions in electronic form and give official authorization of certification to Internet Service Providers (ISPs). The respective framework has now provided Pakistan with a legal backing regarding e-information as well as communication.

Electronic Transactions Ordinance, 2002

The implementation of Electronic Transactions Ordinance, 2002 (ETO) has placed Pakistan in those few countries who understood the importance of cybercrime legislation in early time and provided imperative guidelines and frameworks which enabled and encourage the IT industry to foster at higher standards and spread of e-commerce in Pakistan. The Electronic Transaction Ordinance is of high importance that is necessary in carrying out proper IT growth and considered as a turning point for the Information and Communication Technology development as well as growth in Pakistani context.

Ordinance's Main Aim:

1. Enhanced electronic transactions.

2. Legal and safe trading platforms for sellers as well as buyers.

3. Economic upheaval.

4. Growth in e-commerce, projection of surgical items, sports & leather goods, and textile.

5. Enhanced punishments for offenses involving sensitive electronic systems.

6. Cost reduction strategies for small and medium business enterprises via e-transactions.

Main clauses cover enlisted offenses:

1. Unauthorized interception

2. Spamming

3. Malicious code

4. Misuse of devices

5. Electronic fraud

6. Data damage

7. Criminal access

8. Issue of false certificate

9. Cyber terrorism

10. Spoofing

11. Cyberstalking

12. Misuse of encryption

13. Electronic forgery

14. System damage

15. Criminal data access

16. Damage to information system

17. Attempt and aiding or abetting

18. Provision of false information

19. Waging cyber war

National Response Centre for Cyber Crime

National Response Centre for Cyber Crime (NR3C) formed in 2007 is another initiative taken by the Government of Pakistan to trace cybercriminals and to counter the internet misuse. Regarding the 'Certificate Authority (CA)', the Ministry of Information Technology and Telecommunication (MoITT) formed the Accreditation Council in accordance with the National IT Policy and Electronic Transactions Ordinance, 2002.

This voluntary licensing program aims at promoting high integrity licensed CAs that can be trusted. A Certificate Authority aiming to acquire a license will adhere to a more stringent licensing criteria, which includes:

1. Strict security procedures as well as controls

2. Personnel integrity

3. Financial soundness

Cyber Laws Legislation in Pakistan

The inclination and influence of the internet is surely a positive sign in every society. Simultaneously, it also entails peril for country like Pakistan. Although, IT has become the most essential aspect of everyday life, but the other side is quite alarming too.

According to the Economic Survey of Pakistan 2017, literacy rate of the country is quite low as compared to other countries, i.e., 58 percent. As far as Information Technology education and awareness is concerned, it is even horrible and alarming in the Pakistani context. Thus, it opens the abundance of vulnerability for cybercriminals to exploit. The Prevention of Electronic Crimes Act, 2016 is an excellent achievement by the legislative parliament of Pakistan to curb cybercrime and make ICTs more productive for citizens.

The presence of ICTs and global connectivity in Pakistan has enabled an inclination in the speed and pace of cybercrime activities all around. The reasons are quite obvious, as criminal physical presence is no more needed where he/she has intention to commit crime. Internet speed, convenience, anonymity, and global presence enable digital crimes easier to carry out, like financial crimes, such as ransomware, fraud, and money laundering, as well as hate crimes, such as stalking and bullying.

Cybercriminals target private information as well as corporate data for theft and resale in the cyber criminal's black markets which have grown manifold in cyber space. Attempts to steal financial account, credit card, or other payment card information is one of the biggest threat to financial organization in Pakistan.

John Carlin (1997) opined that potential insecurity is attached with convenience of digital connectivity. Prevention of Electronic Crimes Act, 2016 is an essential and necessary step in the right direction. It not only ensures the security for the IT consumers, but also cover the maximum aspects of crime that can be committed by criminals against society, a group of people, corporate entities, institutions, establishments, and individuals. These crimes may cause mental agony and financial loss, destabilize or undermining the state institutions, or other organizations through the medium of ICTs and networks.

The National Assembly of Pakistan has passed the draft of Prevention of Electronic Crimes Act, 2016 (PECA) on 13th April, 2016. One of the principal reason for drafting the respective Act was to provide a legal framework for attack against computers. Section 3 to 8 of this Act set out enlisted provisions.

1. Unauthorized access to data or Information System (IS).

2. Unauthorized transmission or copying of data.

3. Interference with data or Information System (IS).

4. Unauthorized access to data or Critical Infrastructure Information System (CIIS).

5. Unauthorized transmission or copying of Critical Infrastructure Data (CID).

6. Interference with data or Critical Information System (CIS).

1. **Unauthorized Access to Data or Information System (Article 3)**

"Whoever with dishonest intention gains unauthorized access to any information system or data shall be punished with imprisonment for a term which may extend to three months or with fine which may extend to fifty thousand rupees or with both".

2. **Unauthorized Transmission or Copying of Data (Article 4)**

"Whoever with dishonest intention and without authorization copies or otherwise transmits or causes to be transmitted any data shall be punished with imprisonment for a term which may extend to six months or with fine which may extend to one hundred thousand rupees or with both".

3. Interference with Data or Information System (Article 5)

"Whoever with dishonest intention interferes with or damages or causes to be interfered with or damages any part or whole of an information system or data shall be punished with imprisonment which may extend to two years or with fine which may extend to five hundred thousand rupees or with both".

4. Unauthorized Access to Data or Critical Infrastructure Information System (Article 6)

"Whoever with dishonest intention gains unauthorized access to any critical infrastructure information system or data shall be punished with imprisonment which may extend to three years with fine which may extend to one million rupees or both".

5. Unauthorized Transmission or Copying of Critical Infrastructure Data (Article 7)

"Whoever with dishonest intention and without authorization copies or otherwise transmit or causes to be transmitted any critical infrastructure data shall be punished with imprisonment for a term which may extend to five years, or with fine which may extend to five million rupees or with both".

6. Interference with Data or Critical Information System (Article 8)

"Whoever with dishonest intention interferes with or damages, or causes to be interfered with or damaged, any part or whole of a critical information system, or data , shall be punished with imprisonment which may extend to seven years or with fine which may extend to ten million rupees or with both".

Criticism of PECA

Prevention of Electronic Crimes Act, 2016 is also facing harsh criticism from different political groups, religious groups, INGOs, NGOs, as well as CBOs. According to them, punishment lacks the relevancy to crime, and there are also many ambiguities in the respective act which may cause suffering to users by law enforcers in Pakistan.

ICTs organizations and cybercrime specialist were not taken on-board during the preparation of the act. It is also said that restrictions have been imposed on freedom of expression and access to available information on cyberworld. As cybercrime has a relation to the physical world, many articles in this act are overlapping with previously existing laws. Critics feel that this act can be misused against journalists as well as whistle blowers.

The surveillance criteria does not match the existing act of Fair Trial 2013. How law enforcing agencies will make its implementation possible, while the criminal trial procedure is unclear?

Although critics are claiming that cyberterrorism is not the subject of the bill, therefore terrorism clauses should be removed. While, the world perceives cyberterrorism as the most dangerous threat from intruders. According to a leading United States' newspaper report, i.e., New York Times by David E. Sanger and William Broad (2018), the USA government is even considering the use of   nuclear weapon in the fight against cybercrime.

It is unclear how Pakistani authorities will block or remove online material, and which material will be considered illicit, will law enforcers need court orders to remove online material? Critics are having difficulties in differentiating cyberterrorism and cyberwarfare, that whether it is a category of cybercrime or has some other definite form in the context of Pakistan.

Solutions and Recommendations

1. General public awareness programs should be initiated with regards to cybercrime in Pakistan.

2. During the process of legislation regarding cybercrime in Pakistan, expert opinion should be included, like criminologists, psychologists, sociologists, IT professionals, etc.

3. Pakistan should maintain proper cybercrime data.

4. Victims of cybercrime are large in number, there should be easy access of the victims where they can complain regarding e-offenses.

5. Private companies should develop a strong liaison with the Government of Pakistan regarding the swiftness of their internet approach.

6. Pakistani legal department should be equipped with the latest investigating technologies.

7. Pakistani scholars should discuss cybercrime issue on different forums, specially in print as well as electronic media.

8. To effectively deal with cases of cybercrime, the respective judiciary must be given proper training.

Future Research Directions

The significant areas for conducting future research encompassing cybercrime via engaging qualitative, qualitative, or eclectic approach can be:

1. Cybercrime and freedom of speech in Pakistan.

2. Low conviction rates of cybercriminals in Pakistan.

3. Cyberterrorism and cyberviolence in Pakistan.

4. Cyber security issues in Pakistan.

Conclusion

In the Pakistani context, researches encompassing cybercrime are nominal as the field is relatively new. The easy targets of cybercrime in Pakistan are individuals who are more dependent on technology. To differentiate regarding the categories of cybercrime in Pakistan is not that vivid. There is a difference between the kind of laws that are made in advanced countries and those of Pakistan.

There is no accurate way of understanding how prevalent cybercrime is in Pakistan. There are many reason for this, some of which may be surprising in the context of ordinary crimes. There exists no convenient way to identify how many people have been arrested or convicted of the cybercrime in Pakistan. That is partly, because of the way cybercrime law works in the Pakistani context. Comprehensive cyber laws are a dire need of time in Pakistan, as these laws are in their initial phase.

Cyber laws implementation worldwide is weak, especially in Pakistan because of the unawareness regarding the respective laws. The cybercrime conviction rate is very low, that encourages offenders to commit cybercrime in Pakistan. According to the report of The Express Tribune (2017), in the category of civil justice system, Pakistan ranked 106 out of the participating 113 countries. There are around 1.89 million pending cases in Pakistan (Asad, 2018).

References

Alvarez Technology Group (2018). *2018 Top Cybercrime Facts and Why You Should Care.* https://www.alvareztg.com/2018-cybercrime-statistics-reference-material/

Asad, M. (2018, January 21). Over 1.8 million cases pending in Pakistan's courts. *Dawn.* https://www.dawn.com/news/1384319

Austin, G. (2020). *National cyber emergencies: The return to civil defence.* Routledge. ISBN: 9780367360344

Benson, V., & McAlaney, J. (2019). *Emerging cyber threats and cognitive vulnerabilities* (1st ed.). Academic Press. ISBN-13: 978-0128162033

Bischoff, P. (2018, September 6). *Analysis: How data breaches affect stock market share prices.* from https://www.comparitech.com/blog/information-security/data-breach-share-price-2018/

Bromium, & McGuire, M. (2018, April). *RSA Conference 2018.* San Francisco, USA. https://www.rsaconference.com/events/us18

Carlin, J. (1997, May). A farewell to arms. https://diehard.fandom.com/wiki/A_Farewell_to_Arms?file=A_Farewell_to_Arm s_97.P NG

Cybercrime. (2020). In *Collins English Dictionary.* https://www.collinsdictionary.com/dictionary/english/cybercrime

Cybercrime. (2020). In *Encyclopedia Britannica.* https://www.britannica.com/topic/cybercrime

Cybercrime. (2020). In *Merriam-Webster.* https://www.merriam-webster.com/dictionary/cybercrime

Cybercrime. (2020). In *Oxford Advanced Learner's Dictionary.* https://www.oxfordlearnersdictionaries.com/definition/english/cybercrime

Cybercrime. (2020). In *The Chambers Dictionary.* https://www.cybercrimechambers.com/blog-web-jacking-117.php

Cybersecurity Ventures. *Cybercrime Report, 2017.* https://cybersecurityventures.com/hackerpocalypse-cybercrime-report-2016/

Fuster, G. G., Jasmontaite, L. (2020). Cybersecurity regulation in the European Union: The digital, the critical and fundamental rights. In Christen, M., Gordijn, B., Loi, M. (eds). *The Ethics of Cybersecurity. The* International Library of Ethics, Law and Technology, (21). Springer. https://doi.org/10.1007/978-3-030-29053-5_5

Government of Pakistan. Bureau of Statistics. (2018). *Provisional Summary Results of 6th Population and Housing Census - 2017.* https://bytesforall.pk/

Government of Pakistan. *Investigation for Fair Trial Act, 2013.* http://www.na.gov.pk/uploads/documents/1361943916_947.pdf

Government of Pakistan. Ministry of Finance, Revenue & Economic Affairs. (2018). *Economic Survey of Pakistan, 2017.* http://www.finance.gov.pk/survey_1617.html

Government of Pakistan. Ministry of Information Technology and Telecommunication. (2018). *Electronic Transactions Ordinance, 2002.* http://www.pakistanlaw.com/eto.pdf

Government of Pakistan. Ministry of Information Technology and Telecommunication. (2018). *Prevention of Electronic Crimes Act, 2016.*

http://www.na.gov.pk/uploads/documents/1470910659_707.pdf

Government of Pakistan. *National Response Centre for Cyber Crime (2018).* http://www.nr3c.gov.pk/cybercrime.html

Gillespie, A. A. (2019). *Cybercrime: Key issues and debates.* Routledge. ISBN: 9781351010283

Glenny, M. (2012). *DarkMarket: How hackers became the new media.* NY: Vintage Books.

Hudak, H. C. (2019). *Cybercrime (Privacy in the digital age).* North Star Editions. ISBN-13: 978-1644940815

Hufnagel, S., & Moiseienko, A. (2019). *Criminal networks and law enforcement: Global perspectives on illegal enterprise.* Routledge.

Hutchings, A. (2013). *Theory and crime: Does it compute?.* Griffith University, Australia.

International Monetary Fund (2020). *World economic outlook database.*

https://www.imf.org/external/pubs/ft/weo/2019/02/weodata/index.aspx

Internet World Stats. (2018). https://www.internetworldstats.com/asia/pk.htm

Johansen, G. (2020). *Digital forensics and incident response: Incident response techniques and procedures to respond to modern cyber threats.* Packt Publishing. ISBN-13: 978-1838649005

Jones, C. W. (2005, April). *Council of Europe convention on cybercrime: Themes and critiques.* Workshop on the international dimensions of cyber security. Hosted by Georgia Institute of Technology and Carnegie Mellon University, USA.

Komba, M. M., & Lwoga, E. T. (2020). *Systematic review as a research method in library and information science.* DOI: 10.4018/978-1-7998-1471-9.ch005.

Leukfeldt, R., & Holt, T. J. (2019). *The human factor of cybercrime.* Routledge. ISBN-13: 978-1138624696

Lusthaus, J. (2012). Trust in the world of cybercrime. *Global Crime, 13*(2), 71-94.

Marion, N. E., & Twede, J. (2020). *Cybercrime: An encyclopedia of digital crime.* ABC-CLIO. ISBN-13: 978-1440857348

Marsh, B., & Melville, G. (2019). *Crime, justice and the media.* Routledge. ISBN: 9780429432194

Martellozzo, E., & Jane, E. A. (2017). *Cybercrime and its victims.* Routledge.

Milkovich, D. (2018, December 3). *13 Alarming Cyber Security Facts and Stats.* https://www.cybintsolutions.com/cyber-security-facts-stats/

Nohe, P. (2018, September 27). *Re-Hashed: 2018 Cybercrime Statistics: A closer look at the Web of Profit".* https://www.thesslstore.com/blog/2018-cybercrime-statistics/

Pawson, R., Greenhalgh, T., Harvey, G, & Walshe, K. (2005). Realist review - A new method of systematic review designed for complex policy interventions. *Journal of Health Services Research & Policy, 10*(1), 21-34.

Petticrew, M., & Roberts, H. (2006). *Systematic reviews in the social sciences: A   practical guide.* DOI: 10.1002/9780470754887

Ponemon   Institute.   (2018).   *State   of   Endpoint   Security   Risk.* https://www.businesswire.com/news/home/20181016005758/en/Study-Reveals64-Organizations-Experienced-Successful-Endpoint

Rahi, S. (2017). Research design and methods: A systematic review of research paradigms, sampling issues and instruments development. *International Journal of Economics   & Management Sciences, (6).* DOI: 10.4172/2162-6359.1000403.

Sanger, D. E., & Broad, W. (2018, Jan 16). Pentagon suggests countering devastating cyberattacks   with   nuclear   arms.   *New   York   Times.* https://www.nytimes.com/2018/01/16/us/politics/pentagon-nuclear-review-cyberattack-trump.html

Shehzad, R. (2017, August 26). Global survey: Pakistan ranks 106th in world for justice system. *The   Express   Tribune.* https://tribune.com.pk/story/1491301/global-survey-pakistan-ranks-106th-world-justice-system/

Shenzhen Association of Online Media and China Internet Network Information Center (2015). http://english.sz.gov.cn/ln/201601/t20160121_3452230.htm

Smith. (2018). *Hacking pacemakers, insulin pumps and patients' vital signs in real time.* https://www.csoonline.com/article/3296633/security/hacking-pacemakers-insulin-pumps-and-patients-vital-signs-in-real-time.html

Steinberg, J. (2019). *Cybersecurity for dummies (For dummies computer/tech).* John Wiley & Sons. ISBN: 9781119560326

Summers, S. J., Schwarzenegger, C., Ege, G., Young, F., & Bohlander, M. (2014). *The emergence of EU criminal law: Cyber crime and the regulation of the information society (Studies in international and comparative criminal law).* ISBN-13: 978-1841137278

Summo3000 (2018). *Top 20 Countries Found to Have the Most Cybercrime.* https://www.enigmasoftware.com/top-20-countries-the-most-cybercrime/

Synodinou, T. E., Jougleux, P., Markou, C., & Prastitou-Merdi, T. (Eds.). (2020). *EU internet law in the digital era - Regulation and enforcement.* Springer International Publishing. 10.1007/978-3-030-25579-4

Troia, V. (2020). *Hunting cyber criminals: A hacker's guide to online Intelligence gathering tools and techniques.* Wiley. ISBN-13: 978-1119540922

Victor, L. (2008). Systematic reviewing in the social sciences: Outcomes and explanation . *Enquire 1(1),* 32-46.

Yar, M., & Steinmetz, K. F. (2019). *Cybercrime and society* (3rd ed.). SAGE Publications Ltd. ISBN-13: 978-1526440648

Additional Readings

1. Broadhurst, R., & Chang, L. Y. (2013). Cybercrime in Asia: Trends and challenges. In *Handbook of Asian criminology* (pp. 49-63). New York: Springer.

2. Clarke, R. V. (2012). Opportunity makes the thief. Really? And so what?. *Crime Science, 1*(1).

3. Government of Pakistan. Economic Survey of Pakistan, 2017. http://www.finance.gov.pk/survey_1617.html

4. Government of Pakistan. Electronic Transactions Ordinance, 2002. http://www.pakistanlaw.com/eto.pdf

5. Government of Pakistan. Prevention of Electronic Crimes Act, 2016. http://www.na.gov.pk/uploads/documents/1470910659_707.pdf

6. Government of Pakistan. Provisional Summary Results of 6th Population and Housing Census - 2017. Pakistan Bureau of Statistics. https://bytesforall.pk/

7. Government of Pakistan. Investigation for Fair Trial Act, 2013. http://www.na.gov.pk/uploads/documents/1361943916_947.pdf

8. Imam, A. L. (2012 December). *Cyber crime in Pakistan: Serious threat but no laws!* http://blogs.tribune.com.pk/story/15063/cyber-crime-in-pakistan-serious-threat-but-no-laws/

9. Leukfeldt, E. R. (2014). Cybercrime and social ties. *Trends in Organized Crime, 17*(4), 231-249.

10. Li, Q., & Clark, G. (2013). Mobile security: A look ahead. *Security & privacy, IEEE, 11*(1), 78-81.

11. Lusthaus, J. (2012). Trust in the world of cybercrime. *Global Crime, 13*(2), 71-94.

12. Mohiuddin, Z. (2006 June). Cyber laws in Pakistan: A situational analysis and way. http://www.supremecourt.gov.pk/ijc/articles/10/5.pdf.

13. Momein, F. A., & Brohi, M. N. (2010). Cybercrime and internet growth in Pakistan. *Asian Journal of Information Technology, 9* (1), 1 - 4.

14. National Response Centre for Cyber Crime (NR3C). http://www.nr3c.gov.pk/cybercrime.html

15. Prevention of Electronic Crimes Act, 2016. http://www.na.gov.pk/uploads/documents/1470910659_707.pdf

16. Wall, D. (2007). *Cybercrime: The transformation of crime in the information age.* Cambridge: Polity Books.

17. Wall, D. S., (Ed.). (2001). *Crime and the internet.* NY: Routledge.

18. Webber, C. (2014). *Hackers and cybercrime. Shades of deviance: A primer on crime, deviance and social harm.* London: Routledge.

19. Yar, M. (2013). *Cybercrime and society.* London: Sage Publishing Ltd.

20. Zhang, X., Tsang, A., Yue, W. T., & Chau, M. (2015). The classification of hackers by knowledge exchange behaviors. *Information Systems Frontiers,* 1-13.

Key Terms

1. **Cybercrime:** The use of a computer to commit a crime.

2. **Cybercrime legislation:** The process of making laws regulating cybercrime.

3. **Cyberstalking:** The use of Information and Communication Technology to frighten or harass an individual or group.

4. **Cyberterrorism:** The use of Information and Communication Technology to cause grave disruption or pervasive fear.

5. **Cyberworld:** The world of inter-computer communication.

6. **Cyber security:** Security on the internet.

Chapter 4: Cybercrime Victimization in Pakistan

Abstract

Research studies into cybercrime with regards to the Pakistani context are nominal, as the field is relatively new. Pakistani has a perfect ecosystem regarding cybercrime, as the internet is widely available. The use of social media in Pakistan is increasing exponentially. Adults who carry out online transactions and store important data on their computers are at a high risk of financial theft and hacking in Pakistan. Laws regarding cybercrime exist in Pakistan, but are rarely enforced. The respective culprits usually go largely unpunished in Pakistan. The National Assembly of Pakistan passed the Electronic Crime Bill 2016 after making various amendments to it. Even this bill faced severe opposition in Pakistan. This chapter asses and analyze cybercrime's current state in the Pakistani context.

Keywords: cybercrime, cyberterrorism, cyber world, cyber security, hacking, Pakistan, victims.

Introduction

Anusha Rahman Khan - Minister of State for Information Technology and Telecommunication of Pakistan and member of the committee for development of 'Prevention of Electronic Crimes Act, 2016' (PECA) admitted in a summarized note that, Pakistan has no such laws before to deal comprehensively with cybercrime. She also admitted that, criminal justice legal framework is ill equipped as well as inadequate and to resolve the respective threats of the cyber age. In Pakistan, National Response Centre for Cyber Crime (NR3C) was established in 2007.

It is sometime tempting to downplay cybercrime, painting it always being the action of a lone individual, but while this is true of some crimes, the reality of cybercrime as a whole is very different (Benson & McAlaney, 2019; Johansen, 2020; Troia, 2020; Yar & Steinmetz, 2019). In contemporary era, several thousand groups are dedicated to cybercrime because of the rewards attached to it (Austin, 2020; Gillespie, 2019; Leukfeldt & Holt, 2019). It is clearly evident that as people become more dependent on technology, they become easier targets of cybercrime (Hudak, 2019; Martellozzo & Jane, 2017; Steinberg, 2019), as it also could evolve to bring about new problems (Hufnagel & Moiseienko, 2019; Marion & Twede, 2020). It is also important to realize to what extent it is understood by people that either they are really a victim or can be the victim of a cybercrime (Abaimov & Martellini, 2020; Marsh & Melville, 2019).

It is important to realize to what extent cybercrime is understood by people that either they are really a victim or can be the victim of a cybercrime (Azevedo, 2019; Carlson, 2019; Steinberg, 2019). For example, the sending of emails trying to influence people to enter their bank detail is illegal, but almost every one with an email address will have received an email asking them to confirm their bank details (Bancroft, 2019; Bandler & Merzon, 2020).Another problem is the issue in identifying victims of cybercrime are those situations where people do not know that they have been victimized (Edwards 2019; Graham & Smith, 2019; Hutchings, 2013; Sangster, 2020). Most users of the computer will be aware of the need to install firewall and antivirus software (Littler & Lee, 2020; Schober & Schober; 2019). It is often rare for someone to be told that the program has stopped a virus or potential hack (Kim, 2018; Lavorgna, 2020; Willems, 2019).

"Cybercrime is a crime committed by means of computers or the internet" (Collins English Dictionary, 2020). While according to The Chambers Dictionary (2020), "Criminal activity or a crime that involves the internet, a computer system, or computer technology".

Encyclopedia Britannica (2020) states, "Cybercrime, the use of a computer as an instrument to further illegal ends, such as committing fraud, trafficking in child pornography and intellectual property, stealing identities, or violating privacy. Cybercrime, especially through the Internet, has grown in importance as the computer has".

According to Merriam-Webster (2020), "Criminal activity (such as fraud, theft, or distribution of child pornography) committed using a computer especially to illegally access, transmit, or manipulate data". While, in accordance with Oxford Advanced Learner's Dictionary (2020), "Crime that is committed using the internet, for example by stealing somebody's personal or bank details or by infecting their computer with a virus".

This chapter includes case studies, involving violations of authenticity, confidentiality, as well as human integrity. This is often elaborated through different newspapers as well as TV channels of Pakistan. Their authenticity is checked through multiple reliable sources, like press release or law enforcement agencies of Pakistan, namely the Federal Investigation Agency, National Database and Registration Authority, Provincial Police Department, etc. related to computer-crime and cybercrime division, as well as through multiple relevant and authentic websites.

This involves six cases regarding cybercrime, the outcome of the case, and information based on evidence from the case, as well as the background of criminals. Different case studies provide a wide spectrum of perspectives into what types of cybercrime are getting common, and how the virtual world or cyber space are the area which needs utmost attention to contain and control cyber criminals in the Pakistani context.

Focus of the Chapter

This chapter asses and analyze cybercrime's current state in the Pakistani context. The incidents with victim's name changed are documented in this chapter. The following case studies were chosen because these are the most prominent cases that made headlines and are still in debate across the country. The purpose of this chapter is to assist legislators, corporate executives, law enforcement agencies, academicians, criminal justice officials, IT managers, as well as other professionals.

Research Methodology

This chapter focuses on cybercrime victimization in Pakistan. To this end, qualitative research methodology by using purposive sampling was adopted and six case studies were taken. That is the very reason, it is explanatory in its very nature.

Case Study 1 - ATM Fraud

A sudden overpowering fright spread among the people in Pakistan, when the news was broken regarding Automated Teller Machine (ATM) skimming fraud. The culprits collected information, like ATM card number and PIN code through the installation of skimming devices in ATM machines throughout Pakistan, especially Karachi. Criminals used the personal information for the withdrawal of cash in China and few other countries (Geo News, 2017).

Federal Investigation Agency (FIA) spoke about the matter and confirmed the theft of data and money of around 579 ATM cards users in December 2017. Criminals installed the skimming devices along with hidden cameras in ATMs. Account holders who were unaware of this theft were informed by their respective banks, the agency shared (Geo News, 2017).

Habib Bank Pvt. Ltd., one of the targeted bank also confirmed the theft and installation of skimming devices on four of its ATMs. Criminals installed three devices in Islamabad on different place and one in Karachi. The investigation has been started by FIA under the Prevention of Electronic Crimes Act. The involvement of transnational criminals belong to China has been identified during the investigation. The matter has been discussed on diplomatic level between Pakistan and Chinese officials. The details and evidence of the fraud has been shared by FIA with respective Chinese authorities (Geo News, 2017).

Placing of skimming devices need skills as well as expertise. It is usually used to gather the personal information of debit card user that includes debit card number and personal identification number (PIN). Criminals placed the fraudulent card reading devices which looks same as original on ATMs along with the keypad and a hidden camera which provides them the detailed log.

The offenders used to install the card reader on ATMs, so that the card information can be recorded and the use of camera was helping them to note down the PIN code type by the customers for withdrawing the cash. After recording the activities for few days, they reconciled the data and withdrew the money from other countries. Devices were placed in crowded shopping centres in city, like Karachi.

It was also revealed during the investigation that fraudster made other ATMs dysfunctional on the arena, so that more people used the tempered one. Which ultimately provided them with the maximum number of people's ATM cards information. This sort of cybercrime is not new of its type. According to Group-IB report, cyber criminals had earned more than £10.5 million by hacking the ATM cards information through out the world. It is estimated that offenders have already withdrawn around $2.6 from other parts of the world by this fraudulent use of technology (Cuthbertson, 2018).

The sales of the respective ATM cards and credit cards takes place mostly on the dark web. According to Group-IB findings, its rare to find the sales of ATM card on the dark web from a country like Pakistan. That is why, this is the only reported sales of cards in last six months (Cuthbertson, 2018). In an exclusive TV interview to Dawn News, Mr. Shoaib commented that bank should take the responsibility of this scam. They should have preventive measures to make sure the security of their customers data. The hackers have defrauded a huge amount from card holders accounts. He further said that, this event is an indication for banks to not only upgrade their IT security infrastructure, but to also go beyond strategically to ensure the prevention from future attacks (Zaidi, 2015).

Although, the State Bank of Pakistan has taken the notice and advised all banks to review their security polices to prevent future thefts. It denied about its operations being effected by any of the cyber attack. It is reported that in response to this scam, around six banks have debarred the international use of debit cards temporarily. This news is further endorsed by the chief spokesperson for the State Bank of Pakistan, Mr. Abid Qamar, as he stated that, "It has come to their notice that few banks have suspended the use of cards all over the world except Pakistan" (Geo News, 2017).

Case Study 2 - Hacking Government Websites

Pakistan is also among the effected countries of cyber attacks. Multiple websites have been targeted by black hat hackers. Even an army operated site was attacked, called DDoS attack by the international hackers, as a demo during a live interview to a radio channel. The group of hackers known as, New World Hackers, internationally attacked Pakistan's Frontier Constabulary website on January 10, 2016, while live interview on the Anon UK Radio was in process. It happened just few days after the wave of continuous attacks on government official site (Cuthbertson, 2016).

It is estimated that they almost attacked 60% of the government's official websites. In an statement by the hackers group New world Hackers told that it was not the direct attack from them, but they facilitated Indian hackers, as they were asked to support. The group operates independently, and still takes part in certain operations.

Most of the cyber attacks on Pakistani websites are initiated from India, and it is supposed that it was in response to Pathankot Air Force Base incident, a city in the Punjab state of India, on January 2-5, 2016, where, the death of 14 people was reported. The group further explained that Indians don't attack Pakistani websites for fun, but they take it as a war. The New World Hackers said that they upgraded the capabilities of the Indian hackers worldwide.

Case Study 3 - Illegal Online Drugs

Four members of a narcotics supply gang operating in Defence Housing Authority (DHA) and Clifton, Karachi were arrested in raids carried out by the District South Police (Karachi region) on September 18, 2017 (Perwaiz, 2017). The drug dealers used social media applications, including WhatsApp and Facebook for their transactions and their customer-base was largely comprised of youngsters from high-income localities, said Mr. Javed Akbar Riaz, the Senior Superintendent of Police for District South (Karachi) who supervised the raids.

The officer said teams had been tasked with the investigation after multiple complaints and reports were received regarding the gang's activities in Karachi. The investigators soon found out about the gang's use of Facebook and WhatsApp for communication with customers. Posing as potential buyers, the cops then approached the dealers on the social media platforms and tracked their location.

The team encountered resistance from the suspects, but eventually managed to apprehend two men identified as Ahsan Abbas alias Bilal Shaikh and Taha Kamil and seized a sizeable quantity of hashish. Interrogation revealed that Ahsan was heading the entire operation and the gang consisted in total of eight members.

Acting on information gleaned from the suspects, the police carried out another raid in DHA in which two more gang members, Ashraf Yaseen and Tabassum Hashim, were arrested with more narcotics. As per SSP Akbar Riaz, the gang's modus operandi was based on establishing friendly associations with susceptible youngsters. They (the gang members) would frequent parties and other social gatherings to befriend people. At first, they would offer drugs such as ice, cocaine, and hashish for free. They would wait for the person to develop a dependence on the substance and became a habitual user and then start extorting large sums of money from him or her.

He confirmed the extensive use of social media platforms for transactions and said the gang members provided customers links to their accounts for communication. They were supplying narcotics all over DHA and Clifton. As for the source of the narcotics, they have found out that they were buying the drugs from an area near Shahrah-e-Noor Jehan (Karachi).

Case Study 4 - Hacking into NADRA

The National Database and Registration Authority (NADRA) in Karachi, Pakistan announced a data breach in 2010. Thieves burglarized computers and other equipment. It hasn't been revealed whether disk encryption software was used to protect the contents of the stolen computers (Pakwired, 2016).

There is a possibility of linking to main NADRA servers. The breach happened at a branch office (Shah Faisal Colony Office, Karachi). However, ramifications of the breach may increase, as there is a possibility that the stolen computers could connect to the main NADRA servers, which would allow access to all records nationwide. Many lone hackers have managed to access the vulnerabilities of Pakistani websites, as a Turkish hacker penetrated into the NADRA and FIA official websites. In December 2012, a hacker who is named as Eboz, claimed to access the websites by just applying the simple method of SQL injection, one of the tactics to gain the administrative control access of a website (Pakwired, 2016).

Various countries are also found in spying other countries classified data present on the digital forum. It was revealed in August 2014 that, passport data related to Pakistani citizens which contained sensitive information and even biometric impressions was compromised. It was a breach by CIA and other US intelligence agencies as a part of their undercover project named 'HYDRA' (Pakwired, 2016).

Pakistani secret agencies have even discussed their concern over the unlawful access to data server by foreign secret services. Inter-Services Intelligence (ISI) in August 2014 censure the Israeli secret agency Mossad for their assay to hack sensitive data. Hostile countries, like India and Israel, etc., have been condemned multiple times for their covert attempts by the Government of Pakistan (Pakwired, 2016).

Case Study 5 - FBI's Most Wanted Cyber Criminal

In 2015, Pakistan Federal Investigation Agency (FIA), in a joint effort with FBI, USA, took a person in custody. The arrested cyber criminal was detained in Karachi, he was placed on top 10 most wanted criminals by the USA's government (Zaidi, 2015).

Mr. Noor Aziz Uddin, who unlawfully accessed the systems and deprived the victims of more than $50 million in November 2008 and April 2012. Further details on FBI's official website revealed that he had a reward of $50,000 on his capture. US authorities issued federal warrant for his arrest in several states like New Jersey and New York. He was charged for the act of conspiracy to commit online fraud, identity and personal information theft, and unlawful access to computer systems, etc., (Zaidi, 2015).

He was accused and convicted for establishing illegal telephone exchange which caused heavy losses. The victims were unaware of the respective threat and dangers included individuals, organizations, and government bodies, not only in the United States, but abroad.

Noor, along with a companion Farhan Arshad, unlawfully acquired access to private telephone systems. They crafted a trickery scheme generally known as 'international revenue share fraud'. They were illegally offering long distance telephone calls on expensive rates. This scam costed the real owners huge sum of losses, when they were billed heavily for unused services (Zaidi, 2015).

Case Study 6 - Reporter/Cyber Terrorist

Mr. Shahzeb Jillani is a Pakistani investigative reporter. He has served for Deutsche Welle as well as the BBC. He is currently engaged with Dunya News, a local Urdu news channel in Pakistan. He is accused of cyber terrorism by violating two criminal code provisions and four articles of Prevention of Electronic Crimes Act, 2016. The case is lodged against him by a self-proclaimed 'loyal citizen' on 6th April, 2019. The plaintiff is a supreme court lawyer and he said that he was offended by Mr. Jillani's comment during a television broadcast on 8th December, 2017.

The head of RSF's Asia-Pacific desk, Mr.Daniel Bastard requested, "We urge the court to dismiss these charges against Shahzeb Jillani because, from the legal viewpoint, the case is completely inadmissible".

"Via the all-powerful Federal Investigation Agency, Pakistan's authorities are yet again manipulating the laws in order to silence a journalist who dared to cross a red line by criticizing certain institutions. It is shocking to see how, little by little, case by case, the Pakistani security agencies are tightening their vice in order to intimidate the entire media profession into censoring themselves."

Jillani was later freed on bail, shared with RSF that he is much surprised by the case. He is of the view that his recent story on missing persons, along with his 24th March, 2019 tweet, where he criticized the decision to decorate a senior military intelligence officer who was widely accused of political engineering during the national elections of Pakistan, 2018 are the reasons behind the case against him.

The real reason for the charges was in the run-up to those elections, RSF gave a detailed account of the various methods that the military establishment was using to put pressure on Pakistani media executives in order to impose its viewpoint and to silence reporters.

Jillani also shared with RSF that he has received little support from his news channel management. "The senior management has been told of the case, but their response is very cold". According to RSF's 2018 World Press Freedom Index, Pakistan is ranked 139th out of 180 countries.

Solutions and Recommendations

General public awareness programs should be initiated with regards to cybercrime in Pakistan. It can be done via engaging community as well as CBOs, NGOs, INGOs and cyber vigilantism. During the process of legislation regarding cybercrime expert opinion should be included, like criminologists, psychologists, sociologists, IT professionals, etc. As, in previous legislation, experts were not consulted. Cybercrime data should be maintained according to its nature and severity. It should be shared by Pakistani authorities with other countries. So, Pakistan could learn from the experience of other countries in this sphere.

Students should be educate regarding the vulnerabilities of cyber world via seminars and workshops. Victims of cybercrime are large in number, there should be easy access of the victims where they can complain regarding online offenses. At domestic level, special task force (i.e. cyber police) should be developed to especially ensure online routine checks at the facilities where public internet access is available. Websites should be under strict control regarding any offensive (extremist) content, especially, with reference to race and religious hatred. As, Pakistan is a very fragile state and such content can lead to civil disorder.

Private companies should develop a strong liaison with the Government of Pakistan's officials to ensure their internet services to an optimum level. The legal department in Pakistan should be equipped with the latest investigating technologies. Scholars should discuss cybercrime issue on different forums, specially in print as well as electronic media. Criminological courses focusing on cybercrime should also be included in the regular studies of IT, social science education, law studies, business studies, etc.

E-transactions must be entered via websites that are authentic, and personal data (including passwords) should not be saved on public computers, as it is very unsafe. To effectively deal with cases of cybercrime, the respective judiciary, i.e. Session Court, District Courts, High Courts, as well as the Supreme Court of Pakistan must be given proper training.

Future Research Directions

Significant areas for conducting future research encompassing cybercrime via engaging qualitative, qualitative, or eclectic approach can be:

1. Electronic freedom in Pakistan.

2. Causes of low reporting of cybercrime cases in Pakistan.

3. Cyberterrorism in Pakistan.

4. Countering violent extremism in Pakistan.

5. Awareness regarding cybercrime in Pakistan.

Conclusion

There is no accurate way of understanding how prevalent cybercrime is in Pakistan. There exists no convenient way to identify how many people have been arrested or convicted of the cybercrime in Pakistan. That is partly, because of the way cybercrime law works in the Pakistani context. It was believed earlier that crimes related to cyberworld were very hard to investigate. All cybercrime could be theoretically charged, but as it is unlikely that consecutive sentence would be imposed to all respective offenses occurred before the legislation. It has been observed that there is an increase in people in Pakistan considering themselves to be the victim of a cybercrime.

Cybercrime is one of the major problems with regards to technology in Pakistan, because it is growing by every second in a society where social networking and internet usage is becoming a norm. According to National Response Centre for Cyber Crime (NR3C) data set, in Pakistan, around 20% of the cyber related crimes are reported, the rest of the 80% remains unreported (Manzar, Tanveer, & Jamal, 2016). The forms in which a complaint can be registered are, online, form, fax, in writing and in person. To be able to lodge a complaint, the victim has to be inside Pakistan or the case cannot be entertained.

There is a difference between the kind of laws that are made in advanced countries and those of Pakistan. Cybercrime laws in Pakistan are very complex and even lodging a cybercrime incident is a hectic process. Pakistan is in dire need of making pertinent cyber laws. Pakistan is a developing country, but it has yet to develop cyber-norms, i.e. what is ethical in the Pakistani context and what is not. A low literacy rate as well as low employment rate further add to this dilemma. Therefore, the Pakistani government needs to focus on combating cybercrime, as it is a matter of great concern for upcoming generations in Pakistan.

References

Abaimov, S., & Martellini, M. (2020). *Cyber arms security in cyberspace.* Boca Raton, CRC Press. ISBN: 9780367853860

Austin, G. (2020). *National cyber emergencies: The return to civil defence.* London, Routledge. ISBN: 9780367360344

Azevedo, F. U. B. (2018). *Hackers exposed: Discover the secret world of cybercrime.* Independently published. ISBN-13: 978-1718124615

Bancroft, A. (2019). *The darknet and smarter crime: Methods for Investigating criminal entrepreneurs and the illicit drug economy (Palgrave studies in cybercrime and cybersecurity).* Cham, Palgrave Macmillan. ISBN-13: 978-3030265113

Bandler, J., & Merzon, A. (2020). *Cybercrime investigations: A comprehensive resource for everyone.* Boca Raton, CRC Press. ISBN-13:978-0367196233

Benson, V., & McAlaney, J. (2019). *Emerging cyber threats and cognitive vulnerabilities* (1st ed.). Academic Press. ISBN-13: 978-0128162033

Carlson, C. T. (2019). *How to manage cybersecurity risk: A security leader's roadmap with open fair.* Universal Publishers. ISBN-13: 978-1627342766

Cuthbertson, A. (2016, January 11). Hackers take down Pakistan government websites on live radio. *Newsweek.* https://www.newsweek.com/hackers-take-down-pakistan-government-websites-live-radio-413888

Cuthbertson, A. (2018, November 12). Stolen data from 'almost all' Pakistan banks goes on sale on dark web. *The Independent.* https://www.msn.com/en-xl/asia/asia-top-stories/stolen-

data-from-almost-all-paki stan-banks-goes-on-sale-on-dark-web/ar-
BBPDQdU?li=BBP34wH&ocid=mailsignout

Cybercrime. (2020). In *Collins English Dictionary.*
https://www.collinsdictionary.com/dictionary/english/cybercrime

Cybercrime. (2020). In *Encyclopedia Britannica.* https://www.britannica.com/topic/cybercrime

Cybercrime. (2020). In *Merriam-Webster.* https://www.merriam-
webster.com/dictionary/cybercrime

Cybercrime. (2020). In *Oxford Advanced Learner's Dictionary.*
https://www.oxfordlearnersdictionaries.com/definition/english/cybercrime

Cybercrime. (2020). In *The Chambers Dictionary.*
https://www.cybercrimechambers.com/blog-web-jacking-117.php

Edwards, G. (2019). *Cybercrime investigators* (1st ed.). Hoboken, Wiley. ISBN-13: 978-
1119596288

Geo News. (2017, December 04). Hundreds of Pakistanis lose millions in major ATM
skimming fraud. https://www.geo.tv/latest/170648-hundreds-of-karachiites-lose-
millions-in-major-at-skimming-fraud

Gillespie, A. A. (2019). *Cybercrime: Key issues and debates*, London, Routledge. ISBN:
9781351010283

Graham, R. S., & Smith, S. K. (2019). *Cybercrime and digital deviance* (1st ed.). New York,
Routledge. ISBN: 9780815376316

Hudak, H. C. (2019). *Cybercrime (Privacy in the digital age).* North Star Editions. ISBN-13: 978-1644940815

Hufnagel, S., & Moiseienko, A. (2019). *Criminal networks and law enforcement: Global perspectives on illegal enterprise.* London, Routledge.

Hutchings, A. (2013). *Theory and crime: Does it compute?.* Australia: Griffith University.

International Monetary Fund (2020). *World economic outlook database.* https://www.imf.org/external/pubs/ft/weo/2019/02/weodata/index.aspx

Johansen, G. (2020). *Digital forensics and incident response: Incident response techniques and   procedures to respond to modern cyber threats.* Birmingham, Packt Publishing. ISBN-13: 978-1838649005

Kim, P. (2018). *The hacker playbook 3: Practical guide to penetration testing.* Independently published. ISBN-13: 978-1980901754

Lavorgna, A. (2020). *Cybercrimes: Critical issues in a global context.* Springer. ISBN-13: 978-1352009118

Leukfeldt, R., & Holt, T. J. (2019). *The human factor of cybercrime.* London, Routledge. ISBN-13: 978-1138624696

Littler, M., & Lee, B. (2020). *Digital extremisms: Readings in violence, radicalisation and extremism in the online space.* Cham, Springer Nature Switzerland AG. ISBN13: 9783030301378

Lusthaus, J. (2012). Trust in the world of cybercrime. *Global Crime, 13*(2), 71-94.

Manzar, U., Tanveer, S., & Jamal, S. (2016, June). *The incidence of cybercrime in Pakistan.* 10.13140/rg.2.1.1641.9448

Marion, N. E., & Twede, J. (2020). *Cybercrime: An encyclopedia of digital crime.* Santa Barbara, ABC-CLIO. ISBN-13: 978-1440857348

Marsh, B., & Melville, G. (2019). *Crime, justice and the media.* London, Routledge. ISBN: 9780429432194

Martellozzo, E., & Jane, E. A. (2017). *Cybercrime and its victims.* London, Routledge.

Pakwired. (2016, January 13). How secure are NADRA's critical information systems?. https://pakwired.com/how-secure-are-nadras-critical-information-systems/

Perwaiz, S. B. (2017, September 19). Four held as cops bust gang using social media for drug sales. *The News International.* https://www.thenews.com.pk/print/230859-Four-held-as-cops-bust-gang-using-social-media-for-drug-sales

Reporters Without Borders. (2019, April 16). *Pakistani investigative reporter accused of "cyber-terrorism".* https://rsf.org/en/news/pakistani-investigative-reporter-accused-cyber-terrorism

Sangster, M. (2020). *No safe harbor: The inside truth about cybercrime-and how to protect your business.* Vancouver, Page Two. ISBN-13: 978-1989603420

Schober, S. N., & Schober, C. W. (2019). *Cybersecurity is everybody's business: Solve the security puzzle for your small business and home.* ScottSchober.com Publishing. ISBN-13: 978-0996902267

Steinberg, J. (2019). *Cybersecurity for dummies (For dummies computer/tech).*Hoboken, John Wiley & Sons. ISBN: 9781119560326

Troia, V. (2020). *Hunting cyber criminals: A hacker's guide to online Intelligence gathering tools and techniques.* Indianapolis, Wiley. ISBN-13: 978-1119540922

Willems, E. (2019). *Cyberdanger: Understanding and guarding against cybercrime.* Springer International Publishing. ISBN:978-3-030-04531-9

Yar, M., & Steinmetz, K. F. (2019). *Cybercrime and society* (3rd ed.). SAGE Publications Ltd. ISBN-13: 978-1526440648

Zaidi, M. (2015, February 14). FBI's most wanted cyber criminal arrested in Karachi. *Dawn.* https://www.dawn.com/news/1163584

Additional Readings

1. Government of Pakistan. Economic Survey of Pakistan, 2017. http://www.finance.gov.pk/survey_1617.html

2. Government of Pakistan. Electronic Transactions Ordinance, 2002. http://www.pakistanlaw.com/eto.pdf

3. Government of Pakistan. Prevention of Electronic Crimes Act, 2016. http://www.na.gov.pk/uploads/documents/1470910659_707.pdf

4. Government of Pakistan. Provisional Summary Results of 6th Population and Housing Census - 2017. Pakistan Bureau of Statistics. https://bytesforall.pk/

5. Imam, A. L. (2012 December). *Cyber crime in Pakistan: Serious threat but no laws!.* http://blogs.tribune.com.pk/story/15063/cyber-crime-in-pakistan-serious-threat-but-no-laws/

6. Internet World Stats. (2018).   https://www.internetworldstats.com/asia/pk.htm

7. Investigation   for   Fair   Trial   Act,   2013. http://www.na.gov.pk/uploads/documents/1361943916_947.pdf

8. Leukfeldt, E. R. (2014). Cybercrime and social ties. *Trends in Organized Crime, 17*(4), 231-249.

9. Momein, F. A., & Brohi, M. N. (2010). Cybercrime and internet growth in Pakistan. *Asian Journal of Information Technology, 9* (1), 1 - 4.

10. National   Response   Centre   for   Cyber   Crime   (NR3C). http://www.nr3c.gov.pk/cybercrime.html

Key Terms

1. **Cybercrime:** The use of a computer to commit a crime.

2. **Cyberterrorism:** The use of Information and Communication Technology to cause grave disruption or pervasive fear.

3. **Cyberworld:** The world of inter-computer communication.

4. **Cyber security:** Security on the internet.

5. **Hacking:** To gain unauthorized access to data in a system or computer.

Publisher: Eliva Press SRL

Email: info@elivapress.com

www.ingramcontent.com/pod-product-compliance
Lightning Source LLC
Chambersburg PA
CBHW070842070326
40690CB00009B/1659